D1522420

To:

_____

From:

_____

Date:

_____

the
CAMPFIRE
is calling

90 Warming Devotions

for the Simple Life

DaySpring

LIVE YOUR FAITH

The Campfire Is Calling: 90 Warming Devotions for the Simple Life
Copyright © 2021 DaySpring Cards, Inc. All rights reserved.
First Edition, November 2021

Published by:

21154 Highway 16 East
Siloam Springs, AR 72761
dayspring.com

Written by: Bonnie Rickner Jensen

Cover Design by: Greg Jackson of thinkpen.design

Printed in China
Prime: J6784
ISBN: 978-1-64870-286-0

Contents

Sit, Crackle, and Pop

Let the wise listen and add to their learning.
PROVERBS 1:5 NIV

Sitting around a campfire is one of the simplest ways to draw out our deep-seated desire to slow down, reflect, and listen. The crackle and pop of the wood has a mesmerizing effect that keeps us still and thoughtful. It goes with the flicker of the flames perfectly, creating an experience our senses want to return to again and again.

A whisper from God is worth a thousand sermons, isn't it? It happens when we create a space to listen for a moment and hear what our hearts need to hear to carry us through this battered world. We serve an attentive and personal God who loves every part of us and knows the encouragement we need and when we need it most.

Our busy days can become barriers to being still. They distract us from listening to God, and before we know it, we get to the point of feeling discouraged without really knowing why. Wisdom tells us to *listen*, and to remind ourselves of the unfailing love of our unchanging God. He's with us at all times, and He's ready to speak the words that will teach us and tell us we're loved completely and without condition. Love pours in and insecurities are pushed out.

The key is to *keep* listening and letting love in—as often as we can.

Our spirits are wholly bound to God's, and we need to spend time with Him in order to live in the fullness He wants for us! We can't let the cares of this world put cracks in the trust, peace, and joy we've been given in Him. It's good to plan more time to sit and listen, not only to the crack and pop of firewood but to the loving whispers of our faithful Father.

Dear Father,

I want my spirit to be able to listen

closely and hear clearly. Remind me

to take time for You, to allow love and

wisdom to encourage and guide me.

An Ordinary Way to See
Our Extraordinary Value

Break open Your words, let the light shine out,
let ordinary people see the meaning.

PSALM 119:130 *THE MESSAGE*

We tend to complicate things. We overthink, overworry, and overtake—until we're *overwhelmed*. If we're not careful, we convince ourselves that being in control is comforting. In truth, it only brings a false and temporary sense of security. God's Word sheds light on a different way of living. It's a simple example conveyed in a short parable written for ordinary people to understand. It allows us to see that the *best* way to go through our days is to go to our heavenly Father with every need. "Look at the birds of the air; they do not sow or reap or store away in barns, and yet your heavenly Father feeds them. Are you not much more valuable than they?" (Matthew 6:26 NIV).

There's not a creation on earth more valuable to the heavenly Father than *you*. It's as simple and as significant as that. Every moment we spend striving to get a desired outcome, every ounce of energy we exert trying to make our lives look perfectly in place, and every day we let slip away without putting our absolute trust in God is time we spend forgetting the simple words of our faithful Father: Are you not much more valuable than the birds of the air? Watch and see how I meet their needs.

Everything we have in front of us today—the people we love, the job, the circumstance, the chance meeting, the unexpected interruptions—is seen by the One who promises to provide every single thing we need to get through. We never have to wonder how we're going to handle what God allows. Our value to Him puts our life in the center of His love and at the center of His attention. And His loving response is to be a Father who never forgets the extraordinary price He paid for His most valuable creation. *You!*

Dear Father,
Your faithfulness is my security in an
unsure world filled with unexpected
challenges. I surrender my day to You and
Your loving, always sufficient grace.

Simplifying Life to Gain Strength

In quietness and trust is your strength.

ISAIAH 30:15 NIV

We find ourselves at a time in the world where strength is often measured by physicality rather than spirituality. By no means are physical health and well-being unimportant; they're simply not as important as keeping our spiritual strength a priority. A heart built up in faith has the power to help us stand when it seems everything is collapsing around us. Our *greatest* strength is in the trust that keeps us quiet, at peace, and calm in our innermost being. A trust sustaining us no matter what the circumstances look like. A trust binding us to hope no matter what the headlines read. A trust reminding us of God's faithfulness no matter how long it takes for His hand to move the mountain.

How do we nurture quietness within? How do we develop *strengthening* trust? We do what it takes to simplify our lives. We sit by the fire, we turn off the devices, we realize the gift of the moment we're in. The good in today won't come again. Our heavenly Father has gone ahead of us, so whatever is weighing on us mentally and holding us hostage to the future we can't know or control is *not* from Him. Learning to be present is the best way to prove and strengthen our trust in Him. "For the LORD will go before you, and the God of Israel will be your rear guard" (Isaiah 52:12 NKJV).

Deep breath. Long sigh. God holds us in the palm of His loving, life-giving hand. There's a familiar saying, "Not to spoil the ending, but everything is going to be okay." The truth is it's going to be far better than okay. It's going to be what God has ordered—and there will be love, favor, forgiveness, hope, and a future filled with good things. Good things like warm fires and quiet, trusting hearts.

Dear Father,

Let today be one of strengthening my spirit
by trusting in You. When I want to speak
anything other than faith or favor, help me
stay quiet, look to You, and stand in hope.

Paring Down to Simply Love

Don't complicate your lives unnecessarily. Keep it simple.
I CORINTHIANS 7:29 *THE MESSAGE*

One of the greatest things about camping is being forced to pare down our lives, if only for a few days, to what we absolutely need. And the *best* part of the adventure is ending the day around a campfire with the ones our lives wouldn't be the same without. Camping is comforting that way. It removes what matters least so we can see, by the light and warmth of a fire, who matters most. It's a perfect reminder that God created our hearts to be fulfilled by *who* we love, never *what* we love.

Are there things complicating our lives unnecessarily? Are we stressing about something we can't change? Do we have a list of to-dos that don't really *need* a deadline? What's distracting or detouring us from spending our time with the ones we love most—or loving those who need it most? In I Timothy 2:2 we're urged to pray for everyone, including all those in authority, so that "we may live peaceful and quiet lives in all godliness and holiness" (NIV). God chose each of us to be there for one another—in prayer and in presence. Whatever it takes to pare down the busyness of our days for the ones we love is *worth* doing. If it takes a camping trip and quality time around a campfire to practice putting things in place, then all the better!

We can only live peaceful, quiet lives one day at a time. We can only put things that matter most in their proper place one step at a time. Maybe there's a part of our busy schedule we can rearrange in order to move love into first place. Maybe there's something that can wait so we can shift our attention to a person rather than a project. Maybe having godliness and holiness is taking time to listen to the brokenhearted. It doesn't take a lot—it only takes a decision to put love in its proper place *a little more often* every day.

Dear Father,

Show me how to simplify my life in
ways honoring You and preferring
others. Give me a heart ready to love
first and let go of the lesser things.

God Among Us

*Where two or three gather together
because they are Mine,
I will be right there among them.*

MATTHEW 18:20 TLB

Have you ever had a summer gathering around a bonfire? The great thing about a casual get-together around a fire is the absence of an agenda. Sometimes it turns into a lively night filled with games, conversation, and laughter. Other nights might be more peaceful, marked by the comfort and companionship of friends, the sweetness of silence, and the presence of God. Quietly gazing at a starry sky never disappoints.

God's promise to be *among us* when we gather is what makes gathering beautiful. We realize how much we need each other to get through the challenges of life, how healing it is to hug, and how God builds our support system by choosing the right people to surround us. Nothing is accidental or incidental in a life committed to the Father. God is intentional about His plan and purpose for each one of us.

Let's never stop making time for each other. When possible, let's keep planning time around a fire, under the stars, enveloped in the peaceful and comforting presence of God. We don't know how He'll reveal Himself in the midst of us, whether through an encouraging word we need to hear, a smile we need to see, or the laughter we need to heal our souls. God knows all our needs intimately and meets them abundantly. He's counting on us to get together so He can be *right there among us* and remind us again that the only thing we need to restore our hearts is *Him*.

Dear Father,

Let me be the catalyst for the gathering of friends and the healing of hearts. I want to be used by You to invite people into Your presence and the warmth of Your unconditional love.

A Little Slowdown
Makes a Big Difference

A heart at peace gives life to the body.

PROVERBS 14:30 NIV

When the campfire starts burning and the chairs around it fill and the night air makes us thankful for the warmth we feel, stress loses its grip for a little while. Life takes hold in the peacefulness of these simple times. Our minds stop racing, our hearts start appreciating the slow-down, and we realize again how important these resets are.

God wants us to get into the habit of having hearts at peace through a deeper dependence on Him. He wants us to rest more and worry less. He understands that as dust-derived beings we're going to be lifelong learners because we like to control outcomes. We want to fix problems before we've taken the time to pray and know that God wants us to get involved. We tell ourselves we're being responsible, when sometimes we're being unwilling to relinquish all our cares to the One who loves us with all His heart.

Trusting God takes time, and it also takes *practice*. Our faith gains confidence when we let God be God. When we let go and let God step in, things start to go right! He's at the ready to give us the rest we need. He sees two months down the road and every need met. He watches us through the worry-wasted hours and comes through with the always-faithful answer. He won't leave us for a second or forsake us for any reason.

We shouldn't take lightly the opportunities we're given to slow down. We should treat them with the same respect we do every other goal we set to take care of ourselves. If wisdom says a heart at peace gives life to the body, it deserves our attention. Sit around a fire with friends. Stay a little longer and listen. Give your heart rest, quiet your thoughts, and let your soul get calm enough to hear the still, small voice of God. *He's all the peace and life we'll ever need.*

Dear God,

My life is in Your hands, and my heart finds peace in trusting You. Show me when I need to slow down and how to do it—and help me stay willingly surrendered to Your leading and Your love.

Campfire and Contemplation

We meditate on Your unfailing love.

PSALM 48:9 NLT

ampfire time is great contemplation time. Maybe it's the way the ever-changing flicker of the fire holds our gaze. Maybe it's the combination of color, sound, movement, and warmth that makes us thankful for the simple beauty in front of us. There's no question that every part of being around a campfire brings a comfort we all crave. There are too few things in our lives today that calm our senses, and far too many that stimulate them *continually*.

When everyone finds a seat around the campfire, you can almost hear the collective sigh of our souls: "Aaaahhh . . . a little time to sit and think." Sure, there are thoughts of to-do lists running through our heads, along with appointments, work obligations, and unread emails. It takes some effort to put the daily grind in the back of our minds. But when we do, we allow good stuff like gratefulness, contentment, and childlike joy to come to the forefront. We free up mental space to reflect on how much God loves us and how many reasons we have right now to be *sure* of it.

There are a lot of things in this tangled-up world that are failing—but God's love isn't one of them. His love is what holds us together through it all. When our days start blurring together and we feel like giving up, that's when it's time to stop doing what we think is most important and spend time doing what we know is most *needed*. The pressures of life can force our priorities out of order. It's in the sitting still and the quiet comforts that our strength is renewed. We're reminded that God's love for us is burning brightly, constantly, and unfailingly—and every day is an opportunity to see countless reasons to be *sure* of it.

Dear God,
Your love is the certainty in the midst of
this world's uncertainty. Let Your love
strengthen my heart and open my eyes to see
it everywhere, and *be* it everywhere I go.

Quiet Hope and a Childlike Heart

It's a good thing to quietly hope,
quietly hope for help from God.
LAMENTATIONS 3:26 *THE MESSAGE*

Sometimes the things we hope for are tucked away in such a deep part of our hearts that it feels best, and safest, to keep them there. They're the dreams we trust to God alone. And it's a *good thing* to quietly hope. It's a *good thing* to believe God is working everything out in just the right way, with exactly the right timing, for the most right outcome imaginable—because He *always* is.

How much simpler was it to be carefree as a child? We faced what was in front of us in stride and without question. So fresh from God, our hearts trusted Him fiercely with no thought of what ought to be or what we deserved. Life was ours to enjoy in its simplest, purest form. It's no wonder Jesus told us that *kingdom* hearts look like *children's* hearts. To be like them is to live our days with all the energy, curiosity, and expectancy we possibly can. God is here. God is taking care of us. God is holding every hope we have in the palm of His hands. God is going to bring what is *best*.

Yet, there are downcast days when we don't feel like *anything* is "best." Our wayward emotions encourage us to have more fits and exercise less faith. On days like that, we might need a nap or two. We might need time to play outside. We might need to be around good friends, to laugh, to have our favorite snacks, to hug and be hugged. One thing is for sure: When we stretch out our arms, our heavenly Father won't hesitate to pick us up. His arms never grow weary from the weight of our cares or the magnitude of the hope in our hearts. He's got us, and He'll *always* have us. All we have to do is remember how to put childlike trust in our reigning Champion. All our hopes, dreams, needs, and days are in *good* hands.

Dear God,
Renew a childlike spirit in me today.
Help me trust completely, surrender fully,
and let You lead without fear or question.

God writes the Gospel not in the Bible alone, but also on trees, and in the flowers and clouds and stars.

MARTIN LUTHER

The Simple, Good Things

He fills my life with good things!
PSALM 103:5 TLB

There are a lot of simple, *good* things that come from gathering around a campfire. Warmth. Light. Comfort. Fellowship. Marshmallows. Stargazing. Sitting still. Smiles. Laughter. Stories. Cool night air. The artistic flair of the flames. The more we practice noticing and appreciating the simple, *good* things in our lives, the more they seem to grab our attention. And that might be the *best* good thing of all.

Thankfulness multiplies when we see God's goodness in simpler things. When we appreciate the first deep breath we take in the morning, the way the light comes through the window, the sound of birds singing God's praises at sunrise. The simple things are everywhere. They're always around us. They might not be the things that qualify as special events or standout experiences. They probably won't make it into the stories we retell. These are the day-to-day, moment-by-moment things we often take for granted and let escape our notice. But for our hearts *and* minds' sake, they're always worth seeing.

If joy is our strength, then stacking the simple joys on top of one another might be a great daily endeavor. When they start to build up in our hearts and minds, they begin to spill over into a more sustained feeling of gratefulness. And gratefulness gets God's attention. "Give thanks in all circumstances" (I Thessalonians 5:18 NIV). A continual thankfulness notes a constant trust in the One who loves us most. When we believe His love covers us and His wisdom guides us, nothing falls outside His will for our lives. And His will is working out what is best for us in every way and in every small or significant part of our day.

Dear God,
Let today be one of seeing and appreciating
the simple things, so that every simple
joy will build strength in me.

Little Things Make Brighter Days

We have become gifts to God that He delights
in, for as part of God's sovereign plan we were
chosen from the beginning to be His.

EPHESIANS 1:11 TLB

A campfire doesn't begin with the biggest hunks of wood on the pile. We need small twigs. We need kindling material that lights easily and burns quickly. They create the heat needed to give the bigger pieces time to start, and stay, burning. The little things lead to the best thing—a fire to warm us, relax us, and light the darkness around us.

Maybe the best way to start our best day is with a few little things too. A simple prayer: *Thank You, Father.* A quick observance: *What a beautiful morning.* A little truth: *I'm a gift God delights in.* In the beginning, God *chose* you. He knew you'd be one of the ways His love would shine brightly in this world. He knew you were going to *keep* His light burning for all to see. *Your life is one of God's best things.* It's up to you to give the fire in you what it needs to stay burning brightly. A good way to do that is to stoke it with little things that make a big difference.

Every single one of those little things is fueled by love. It's important to be thankful for, and notice, God's love for us every day. It's equally important to show His love to others. Nothing else will make a brighter impact. We can begin in little ways: a simple *I love you* when our loved one isn't acting all that lovable; a handwritten note, even if it's only a few life-giving words; or a text for no reason, except to remind someone they're valued and appreciated.

Love is the way to keep God's light in this world from going out—and it's *always* the best way to fan it into flame.

Dear God,
Your love is both seen and shown in simple
ways. Give me the heart to begin with
little things that make a big difference.

Making Time for a Quiet State of Mind

We can live in peace and quietness, spending our time in godly living and thinking much about the Lord. This is good and pleases God.

1 TIMOTHY 2:2–3 TLB

We can all agree that sitting around a campfire nurtures a feeling of peace and quietness in us. It's one of the simple pleasures that draws us into a simpler state of mind.

There are few activities in our lives that lend themselves to quieting our minds and "thinking much"—about *anything*. More often we're trying to wrangle the tangle of pressures, obligations, worries, and schedules cluttering our thought life.

It's good to declutter. And it's *especially* good to reflect on what God is doing in our lives. We can imagine how pleasing it is to Him when we stop the mental rush for a little while and *think* about it. Dwelling on how many times He's come through for us builds our trust in Him. Remembering the times He's done more than we expected creates a deeper well of appreciation in us. Making time to *think much about the Lord* is a *necessary* good thing if our lives are going to produce good fruit.

Another great reason to quiet our minds and think about God's goodness is to allow His peace to settle in. It's getting increasingly difficult to find hope in what we see. In a world heavy with strife and division, we need to put more of our focus, more of the time, on our only hope. God alone is the One who can fill us. In Him, there's no running empty on what keeps us going. Hope. Joy. Peace. Strength. Courage. Truth. It's *all* we need, and it's *all* in Him.

Dear God,
I look forward to making more time
to quiet my mind to think about You
and the things You've done and are doing
in my life. Your actions are driven by
love, and my heart fills with gratefulness
and hope when I remember them.

A Simple, Full, and Fearless Trust

The Lord protects the simple and the childlike.

PSALM 116:6 TLB

Walking hand in hand, depending deeply, trusting fully. These are the ways of a child with a parent. Children keep it simple because it's all they know. Growing up has a way of shifting us into the mindset of believing it's enviable to be self-sufficient. In truth, it's not what God wanted or intended. We will *never* outgrow being His children.

The further along we get on the journey of our lives, the wiser we become. We discover that with God, it's good to do some reverting to a childlike dependency. We find out how freeing it is to simply take God at His word. We learn how beneficial it is to cast every care at His feet and *leave* it there. We realize that by trusting Him completely, and patiently, we end up in the best place we can be. God is first a Father, and to our blessing and reward, He's *a perfect* one.

It's comforting to know everything that comes to us flows from and through His love. When our life is hard, God's heart hurts too, but He'll give us every ounce of strength we need to get through. When we wander away from Him, His grace reaches far and wide to guide us back into His arms.

When we exhaust our resources trying to meet our needs, He loves us patiently and puts the provision in place at the right time. The Lord protects the simple and childlike because they *know* they need Him and they rely on Him fully and fearlessly.

Wouldn't it be wonderful to live *without a doubt* in His unfailing love today? To rest in the absolute *certainty* He's protecting us with the fervency of a Father's heart? We can because He *is*—and the childlike trust is up to us.

Dear God,

Give me a heart that is secure in You today.
You've gone ahead of me, You know every
need, and You see every challenge. Thank
You for being my unfailing Father.

Keeping It Simple

*He gives me new strength. He helps me
do what honors Him the most.*

PSALM 23:2-3 TLB

Trusting Jesus means our strength comes in much simpler ways than we might've fallen into the habit of believing or doing. We're daily bombarded with messages of becoming mentally stronger, physically fitter, and more spiritually centered. There's no question whether the health of every part of our being is essential to our wellness; it absolutely is. Jesus simplified the process for us. "Love the Lord your God with all your heart and with all your soul and with all your mind and with all your strength" (Mark 12:30 NIV).

It starts with love and culminates in strength. Loving God with *every* part of who we are brings us to the strongest version of ourselves, developing in us a deeper love for Him. From a heart standpoint, loving God means letting Him in with full surrender. There's no hiding the messiness in there. He sees it all. The transparency is for *our* good, because our souls suffer (as do our minds) when we're afraid to be authentic and open with our heavenly Father. When we have the courage to share all our areas of weakness, humility al-

34

lows us to see all the things God wants us to do—and every one of them will lead to our wholeness and well-being.

Love is the hope, the healer, and the highest goal we can pursue for living a simple and fulfilling life. When our hearts, souls, and minds are set on loving God, He gives us the strength to do what honors Him most. And that brings us right back to love. What honors Him most is *being* His love to others. A simple life is marked by simple actions that reveal the love of God. Opportunities will present themselves every day, and if we let God into every corner of our hearts, love will reveal itself in everything we do.

Dear God,

Give me the strength to love You most

and the courage to love others every

chance I get with every day You give.

Prepared with Truth to Be the Light

You are the world's light . . .
glowing in the night for all to see.

MATTHEW 5:14 TLB

An enjoyable, long-burning campfire needs the proper attention to be successful. It takes the right elements and consistent tending to keep it going. Kindling, patience, and a stack of firewood are a few of the essentials. Being prepared makes relaxing around the fire happen a lot simpler, and a lot sooner! If the preparations aren't made or the right elements aren't at hand, it's much harder to get to the desired outcome.

Likewise, our hearts benefit from being prepared to love and serve God every day. Prayer, praise, and a stack of scriptural truths are a few of the essentials. When our day starts with thoughts of defeat before we even get out of bed, we need to have truth at the ready to stoke the fire of God's Spirit within us. Truth is the only thing that extinguishes the lies that come against us. Truth is the only thing that allows the Holy Spirit to burn brightly and lead the way. Truth is the only thing that *keeps us going*.

If a thought comes that doesn't line up with something God *has* said, or sound like something God *would* say, it can't be given the time to ignite another thought. It has to go—and we have to get into the habit of throwing truth on it quickly to put it out. Lies will simmer if we let them. Lies will keep flaring up if we listen to them. We can be a light in this world if we stay *prepared* to shine, and we can continue to shine brightly if we give our source of light the proper attention.

Dear God,

You see my heart, and You purify it with Your truth and love. Prepare me today to be a *light* in this world. Every good thing in me is because of the unfailing grace in You. Keep me going, Father, and let me shine brighter than ever.

Sensing the Sacred
in Small Moments

Keep your lives simple and honest.
ZECHARIAH 8:17 *THE MESSAGE*

Do any of us really mind the sticky, messy, melty part of making s'mores? It's part of the campfire experience, isn't it? As is dropping a marshmallow or two in the fire, noticing how each person likes to toast their marshmallow, and getting yours just the way you want it no matter how many attempts it takes. The simple joy in simple things is a comforting reminder that God is in the small moments as well as the big ones in our lives, maybe even more palpably.

Big moments and big events garner a great deal of attention on their own, but the small, quiet moments give us a chance to truly rest in the presence of God. And it feels *good*. The kind of good that reassures us we're held closely in a world spinning wildly away from the comforts of a simple life. Everything is moving faster, distracting us further and pulling us farther from the God who loves us so sweetly, gently, and *completely*. No accomplishments needed. No criteria to meet. No amount of followers necessary to pique His interest or get His attention. We have His *undivided* attention every moment of every day. And that is simply *all* we need to be happy, fulfilled, and certain of our infinite value.

Sure, there will be sticky parts in life we'd rather avoid. Messy things we'd like to bypass. But each one is a part of the earthly experience God scripted for our unique stories. No two are exactly the same, and not one is more important than another. Maybe today we can be brave in God's embrace—even if the marshmallow falls in the fire . . . even if our hands get messy doing things we *have* to do but that are *hard* to do . . . even if our hearts feel like melting under the pressures of discouragement or disappointment. Maybe today we can sense God in a big way through the small, quiet moments.

Dear God,

Where I am, You are. Open my heart and my eyes to see Your purpose in the messy, the mundane, and the miracles in every moment.

The Power of the Parable

Speak encouraging words to one another.
Build up hope so you'll all be together in
this, no one left out, no one left behind.

1 THESSALONIANS 5:11 *THE MESSAGE*

Sitting around a campfire creates a perfect atmosphere for storytelling. Jesus did much of His teaching through the parables He told. He knew conveying God's love and truth through a simple story was the best way to make it relatable. In the same way, we can see our lives and our common struggles in the stories people share with us. When they talk about things God has walked them through or ways He carried them during a seemingly impossible time, the picture of how God works in our lives becomes clearer. We gain confidence and understanding. We see how similar our trials are and how hopeful we can be in God's unfailing love and faithfulness. He *never* changes.

Troubles can tempt us to become isolated. Sometimes our response is to hunker down, be alone, and avoid every activity—and every campfire invitation—until the storm is over. If God is with us, after all, why do we need to be in the storytelling presence of friends, family, and neighbors? *Because love lifts us up through the encouragement of oth-*

ers. Being with those who love God and care about us, even when we don't feel like it, often becomes the gift we weren't expecting.

So the next time it seems like a good idea to curl up in a ball and roll into a corner, it's probably a better time to reach out and get our soul-weary selves to a gathering. A place where we'll find a warm fire, a good friend (or friends), the peaceful presence of God, and some brave stories told. Courage is contagious when God's faithfulness is the place it's coming from—and it's a *powerful* thing to catch.

Dear God,

Give me the strength and willingness to surround myself with people You've chosen to help me stand. Thank You for giving me the courage I need through the encouraging words of others.

A Simple Effort Makes
an Eternal Difference

*When we get together, I want to
encourage you in your faith,
but I also want to be encouraged by yours.*

ROMANS 1:12 NLT

We're better together. Life is better when we spend time together. Days are more fulfilling when we're there for one another. Sometimes the most memorable evenings happen when we've done the least to prepare for them. Spur-of-the-moment backyard campfire nights are great simplifiers. When we eliminate time to worry about having everything perfectly prepared, we give ourselves time to concentrate on the real reason for being together. *Our hearts need the boost.*

We need to know we're not alone in the challenges we face. It's good for us to laugh about how imperfectly we're doing the tough days, how we're stumbling over the same obstacles, and how grace is the only thing getting us through it all. God is about friendship, compassion, and connection. As a loving Father who knows how to take care of every part of His creation, He loves to see us leaning on each other. Being made in His image makes our human connections an important reflection of the love that formed us. A weakness we see in ourselves might be a strength we see in someone else, and being around them is a great way to be encouraged, to become stronger, and to be more like *love* is meant to be.

It's okay to lighten up on the pressures of perfect hospitality every now and then, invite some friends over, and open the door to a wonderful exchange of encouragement. It's good practice for putting relationships first—they're the only part of the effort making an *eternal* difference.

Dear God,

I want my relationships to be a priority. Every one You've given is a gift to be thankful for, to nurture, and to value. Thank You for showing me all the ways I can be an encouraging vessel of Your kindness and love.

Shining with Simplicity

As we obey this commandment, to love one
another, the darkness in our lives disappears
and the new light of life in Christ shines in.
1 JOHN 2:8 TLB

Love in action dispels the darkness in our lives. When we start to feel dissatisfied, feel discouraged, or see our hope dimming, it's time to make sure we haven't turned our attention inward and neglected to let the light of Christ—through love—shine *outward*. Our happiness surges when we make the time and effort to love the people in our lives. We're filled with light that God never intended to keep hidden. Love turns on the power!

The ways to show love aren't limited to certain things or measured by an amount we have to give in order to make an impact. Love beams brightly in simplicity. A hug. A smile. A handwritten note. A phone call. A cup of coffee. A hello. A thank-you. A knock on a neighbor's door to make sure they have what they need. A word of encouragement, kindness, or hope. It all matters, and it all makes us feel like we matter.

A simple life of loving people outshines any fame or fortune attainable in this world. The latter will one day be snuffed out, while the former will light eternity. Little acts of love reveal a very *present* God. They whisper, *You're not alone.* They remind, *You're valuable.* They encourage, *You're going to make it through this.* They affirm, *God sees you.*

Today we can choose to shine for all to see, knowing the most beautiful part of loving others is pointing them to the One who *is* love. We're simply blessed to be holding the light.

Dear God,

Don't let an opportunity pass for me to shine the light of Christ into the lives of everyone around me. I want to flood the world with Your love and reflect the light I've been given through grace.

As you know
Him better, He will
give you, through
His great power,
everything you
need for living a
truly good life.

II PETER 1:3 TLB

Taking Time to Become Spiritually Seasoned

*Run after mature righteousness—faith, love,
peace—joining those who are in honest
and serious prayer before God.*

II TIMOTHY 2:22 *THE MESSAGE*

If you've been in charge of a campfire, or been around one often enough, you know that different kinds of wood burn differently. Some wood burns slowly, some quickly. Some wood creates more heat. Some wood releases a pleasant fragrance while burning. Some wood smokes too much, which isn't pleasant at all. The right wood makes all the difference in the enjoyment of a campfire. Seasoned firewood is best. Using it is the wisest way to have a steady, warm, cozy fire. But seasoning wood takes time.

In the same way, our lives burn brighter and more effectively in a dark world when we become *spiritually* seasoned. Getting there means spending time learning truth and knowing God. One of the rewards of growing close to Him is growing more aware of what we were created to be and what we're here to *do*. Our purpose isn't interchangeable. It's as unique as we are. Isn't that something to get excited about every day?

Our path, from morning until night, is mapped out for God's glory. It doesn't matter if we leave the house every morning or spend most of our days within its walls. It doesn't matter if we travel to the other side of the world or never get out of the city we live in. Our steps are ordered by the God we serve. He called us by name to be a steadily burning reflection of His love. He chose us individually to be a pleasant fragrance of His grace. A seasoned spirit exudes love, joy, peace, patience, kindness, goodness, faithfulness, gentleness, and self-control—and that makes *all* the difference in how enjoyable we are to be around.

Dear God,
Let me be content with my days and the things You've called me to do. Your purpose for every part of my day is a valuable chance to be a bright, loving, and pleasing reflection of You.

A Flicker or a Flame?

*The Holy Spirit, God's gift, does not
want you to be afraid of people,
but to be wise and strong, and to love them.*

II TIMOTHY 1:7 TLB

How do we want the love of God to look in our lives today? Do we want it to flicker, being barely visible to those around us? Or do we want to stir it into a blaze, being unmistakably strong, bold, and irresistible? Love makes us happy to be alive, whether we're on the giving or receiving end of it. Love is God in our presence. Love reminds us of our infinite value, our irreplaceable spot in the world, and the absolute assurance that we have a gentle, kind, compassionate Father holding us steady—even when all the world feels like it's shaking apart.

There are times when it's difficult to muster the courage we need to give, when everything in us feels like we need a love fest thrown *for* us, not through us. It feels like our tank is empty and our energy is depleted. And sometimes it's just plain hard to hang in there when trials are pulling us in a downward trajectory. But we can do this because God is with us. His immovable, unstoppable, unquenchable life is in us. With His never-ending life comes His never-changing love. There's nothing that can keep us down when we're looking up!

Today we'll trust in the love that has the power to lift and lead us. One loving act can point one searching heart to the One who gave His life for them. The wisdom and strength God gives is for the sake of loving this world back to Him. We're chosen, called, and equipped to do it. All we need are the gifts He's already given through the grace that's *always* enough.

Dear God,

Every good and perfect gift comes from
You. Help me use the gifts You've given
to show Your love to others. Love can
open a heart and light the way to You.

Calmed and Quieted

I do not concern myself with great
matters or things too wonderful for me.
But I have calmed and quieted myself.

Dwelling on things we can't control or change is the easiest way to make our lives more difficult and the simplest way to drain our energy. We need our spiritual energy to focus on the good things God has for us and the right things He wants us to do. Mental crowding can cause spiritual congestion. We can't trust God and worry at the same time. Trusting leaves the need to Him. Worrying transfers the weight of it to our hearts and minds. It's a heaviness neither was designed to bear.

Living simply comes by trusting fully that God sees us, knows us, and loves us without condition. It's believing we don't have a thing to worry about. There isn't a single part of us equipped to handle stress. God created us to know that we need Him and to learn how to depend on Him. His desire is for us to love Him completely, surrender fully, and allow Him to lead. When we believe wholeheartedly that God is a constant, loving, and active part of every step we take, peace pours in to submerge every fear.

A calm soul sees more clearly the answer God has for the problem. A quieted heart knows more confidently the power God has to make a way where there is no way. In God's hands our lives are in the best place they can be. To think and overthink about fixing all the things that keep our minds busy and our bodies awake at night is to forget how much God loves us. He can never, *ever* fail. What a comfort to be able to turn to Him without reservation, knowing His grace is there without hesitation.

Dear God,

It's up to me to put my trust in You. Fill

my soul with reminders of all the ways

You've come to my rescue in the past

and been a faithful, loving Father.

The Right Focus

Fix your attention on God.
You'll be changed from the inside out.

ROMANS 12:2 *THE MESSAGE*

Simplifying where we focus our attention can prove to be *anything* but simple. Especially at a time when we go through our days tethered to a phone, which is essentially a computer connecting us to the entire world. That's a lot of temptation for us to fix our attention on the wrong things. We look down and lose track of time. Before we know it we've seen too much bad news and read too many negative comments.

God is always the *right* focus of our attention. We get the proper perspective in a hurry because love is influencing how we see things. We see the person in front of us, not as someone testing our patience, but as someone needing a dose of unfailing love. We see the challenge we face, not as a threat, but as an opportunity to grow our faith. We see the fear, not as a force we can't overcome, but as a reason to lean into the strength, hope, and comfort sustaining us.

God is about the heart changes that lead us to our higher place. "From the ends of the earth I call to You, I call as my heart grows faint; lead me to the rock that is higher than I"

(Psalm 61:2 NIV). God's focus is on *us* every moment of our lives. He designed us in perfect and *purposeful* detail. He uses every single thing in our lives to move us closer to Him if we choose to see it. The distractions are all ours. His love is focused entirely on us.

Let's choose to respond to the *longing* God has for us to look to Him for everything we need. We're going to see Him come through mightily—with more than enough.

Dear God,

I'll fix my focus on You today and see

every moment as a gift You'll use to

make my heart more like Yours.

Simple Trust One Day at a Time

Don't be anxious about tomorrow.
God will take care of your tomorrow too.
Live one day at a time.

MATTHEW 6:34 TLB

It's such a simple instruction. *Live one day at a time.* Why are we so good at complicating it? It's physically impossible to live at any other pace, but *too* possible to live ahead mentally. Our thoughts should be well-guarded, like our hearts. Thoughts that go against what God says weaken our ability to live in the present. They can make us feel bad about what we did yesterday, last week, or last year, when God has forgiven and forgotten it. Anxious thoughts can make us feel panicked over what might be and what might not ever happen.

God will take care of you. God will take care of your tomorrow. God will take care of the next chapter of the story He's *already* written for you. What an amazingly *freeing* thought that is! Following the story line is as simple as believing the Author . . . and as difficult as getting the pen out of our own hands. It's human to think about tomorrow. We feel responsible in doing so. But let's stop and think about everything in our life *today*. Right now. To invest ourselves fully in as many moments as we can is an exercise in the discipline of a simple life, marked by simple trust, leading to increased spiritual strength.

God loves being a Father! Learning to rely on Him is honoring, glorifying, and *good*. It's a form of worship and a proclamation of praise. Every time we calm a fear by casting a care on Him, it's like whispering, *Thank You, Father*. Each time we stay in the moment by abandoning a worry, it's like saying, *I trust You, Father*. And when we live one day at a time with a joy the world can never give, it's like exclaiming, *I love You, Father!* God's provision for our tomorrow is our peace for today. And when it comes to living happily, there's no better way.

Dear God,

Thankfulness, trust, and joy

will be my praise to You today.

I'll rest in You and live in the moment.

Let Your Light Shine!

Don't hide your light! Let it shine for all.
MATTHEW 5:15 TLB

How we arrange the wood on a campfire is important to how well the campfire burns. It takes a lot longer for it to become the brightly burning, heat-generating, enjoyable-to-be-around fire if the wood is piled on without thought. The wood needs air to burn. It needs to be stacked carefully and with intention. It's worth taking the time before lighting it because the fire will go out quickly if it's not given a good foundation.

It's necessary for us to take the time and care to give our lives a good foundation too. How we arrange our priorities determines how well the light of God shines through us. Becoming the brightly shining, love-generating, desirable-to-be-around child of God takes being deliberate about what we put first, or rather *who* we put first. Rushing through our days without thinking about what our spirit needs will cause our light to go out quickly.

We need the breath of God's Spirit to keep us going. Making a difference in the lives of those around us begins with being grounded in truth and determined to love. God will surround us with people who need the comfort we have to give. We're created to shine with the light that illuminates the heart of Jesus.

Today will be full of chances. Chances to put a spotlight on love. Chances to exude the warmth of kindness and the spark of hope. Chances to radiate the compassion and tenderness toward others that God so generously shows us. We might be the only bright spot in someone's day—let's be a *brilliant* one!

Dear God,
Keep me grounded in You, Your truth, and
Your light. Show me how to shine Your
love into every person in my life today.

Lighting Our Little
Spot in the World

His life is the light that shines through the darkness.

JOHN 1:5 TLB

We don't have to be close to a campfire to see its bright yellow glow on a dark night. The light it gives can be seen from a distance. What if our lives could be as effective at lighting up this dark world? We're created so they *can* be. Everything we do in love has a lasting effect. The light of a single act of love goes a long way. If we'd pile them up day after day, we'd build a bonfire of love that would overcome every dark corner on this earth. God would see its bright yellow glow all the way from heaven and smile big at the sight of it!

What are some simple ways to light up the world with love? A smile, an I'm sorry, an outstretched hand, a servant heart. Standing next to someone, sitting quietly with someone, speaking an encouraging word to someone, saying "I love you" to someone who might not hear it often enough. There are a thousand ways to spread love and as many different opportunities to do it in each of our lives.

We can be confident that God is the great director when it comes to spreading love in the world. He has a part for each of us to play, and we're created perfectly for it. The people in our lives, the people we meet, the places we live, the jobs we do—every area presents unique ways to communicate God's love through the uniqueness of who we are. A simple life is one of simply knowing we're right where we're supposed to be, and not one life or act of love is more important than another.

Let's gather around the idea of lighting up our little spot in the world by looking for chances to do little acts of love everywhere we go. Whatever we do, big or small, brightens the place we're in and drives the darkness out.

Dear God,
Let Your lovelight shine through me today.
In the ordinary things, in the unexpected
things, and in everything You planned
for my life. There are no coincidences
when I surrender all I do to You.

There Is Purpose in Rest

Remember, your Father knows exactly what
you need even before you ask Him!

MATTHEW 6:8 TLB

There's something special about having a campfire with friends late in the fall, when the chill in the air hints at winter. Everyone knows spending time outside will soon give way to spending a lot more time inside. The fresh air feels exhilarating, the warmth of the fire invokes a little more gratefulness, and the conversations go a bit longer.

The cold months pull us into our homes, and we find ourselves falling into hibernating tendencies. Savoring the simple feels easier. A bowl of homemade soup tastes gourmet. Blankets feel softer. The fireplace is especially comforting. While we're cozied up in simple survivor mode, it can sometimes be easy to think we should be doing more. We can think our lives are passing by in the uneventful days of the ordinary and making no real impact.

God has purpose in rest. He showed the importance of it after creating all that we see and all that we are. He put it in His top ten ways to express our love for Him. He knew we needed time to simply *be*. So let's do it. Rest without regret. Rest without letting the rigorous schedule of life interrupt. Rest with every fiber of our being, knowing His love is around us, preparing us for what's ahead. We don't always have to be doing, going, moving, or planning to feel like we're living. Our life is in God alone. The simplicity of that truth is encouragement enough to face our days, however they unfold, with joy, confidence, and peace.

God knows our every need, both spoken and unspoken. He hears the silent cries of our broken hearts as clearly as He hears the shouts of our frustrations and fears. We're cared for constantly and completely by a love that will never hesitate to be all we need.

Dear God,
I'll rest in You and Your perfect love
today. Nothing can separate me from
it, nothing is stronger, and nothing can
stand against what You have planned!

Becoming a More Beautiful Reflection

Keep company with Me and you'll
learn to live freely and lightly.
MATTHEW 11:30 *THE MESSAGE*

The flames in a campfire are constantly changing from one vibrant hue to another, each one adding dimension and beauty. The circumstances in our lives are ever-changing too, each one adding growth and beauty as we learn to trust God more deeply. With every challenge, disappointment, unexpected loss, or new beginning, we make a choice to walk through it with trust or struggle through it in fear. Peace is the outcome of trusting God. Worry and stress find their home in fear. God understands both reactions—and He'll hold us closely through the faith or the fear.

A simple life is marked by a courageous response to the things God chooses and uses to shape us. There are no surprises for Him on our journey. Our calmness is in the certainty of His faithfulness. *It will not waver*. We're never alone, even in the hours when our pain is overwhelming and our hope is hidden in the hurt we feel. It's then that God is closest to us—and He comes close to *pick us up*. We don't always have to feel strong or be strong. We only have to believe that God is the strength we need when our strength is gone.

Mornings are a good time to set our thoughts on what God has done for us in the past and get hopeful about what He's going to do in our future. His love has good things lined up. Our mandate is *simple trust*. It's taking every thought captive to the truth: No matter what this looks like, God sees me overcoming. With Him I will not fear the outcome. Because of Him I have the strength I need. For Him, I will grow through this, and my life will continue becoming a more beautiful reflection of love, kindness, patience, and joy.

The world needs the beauty of you today—and God sees more than *anyone* how truly beautiful you are.

Dear God,

Becoming a clearer reflection of Your love
is the desire of my heart. Everything in
my day is by Your design. Give me courage
to go through it and grow through it.

I am
with you;
that is all
you need.

II CORINTHIANS 12:9 TLB

Simple Things to Slow Us Down

I've kept my feet on the ground,
I've cultivated a quiet heart.
PSALM 131:2 *THE MESSAGE*

In the haste of our days we neglect to do sweet, simple things for ourselves. Things like taking a stroll, squeezing in a nap, sitting down to sip our favorite tea (with our favorite cookie of course). We should never take for granted how the little pleasures help us slow down. It's hard to appreciate a simple life if we never incorporate the simple things into our days. Sometimes just taking a moment to look out a window at the birds, who haven't a care in the world, reminds us how to live.

"Look at the birds, free and unfettered, not tied down to a job description, careless in the care of God. And you count far more to Him than birds" (Matthew 6:26 *The Message*).

Oh, to get into the habit of being careless in the care of God. To stay mindful of how much He values you. There isn't a person on this earth who means more to Him than you do today. Everything in your life matters as much to Him as it does to you. You don't have to think about how every detail of your day is going to go or if it will work out according to plan. Whatever you need will be there, and what doesn't happen wasn't meant to!

One thing is for sure: God saw today before the sun came up. There might be some things in it you didn't expect, but if there are, you can handle them with a carefree heart knowing *all* is in the care of God. If the schedule changes because a friend calls and needs to talk, welcome the blessing of *being* a blessing. We're created for each other, to love each other, and to help each other get through life's harsh places.

It's a good day to free our minds from the rigidness of lists and expectations and allow God's grace to walk us through. Nothing forced, nothing feared, and nothing getting in the way of what God planned and the good He'll bring out of it.

Dear God,

Living without a care is the path You want
me to choose and enjoy. I can be better
for the people in my life when I trust
You're always working out what's best.

The Power and Purpose in a Simple Life

If you follow Me . . . living light will flood your path.

JOHN 8:12 TLB

The embers of a campfire glow and radiate heat long after the flames go out. Stir them and it's possible to restart the fire. When we let God's love move through our lives into the lives of others, the feeling of gratefulness, the sense of worthiness, and the warmth of kindness stay with them long after the love is given. When we make someone feel loved, it has a wonderful and lasting effect.

There are a lot of distractions in our lives that can lead to a lot of missed opportunities to love other people. We don't notice what's going on around us and maybe don't "listen" to the still, small voice within. If God is in it, love and kindness will be in it too. In a world where we look at screens more often than into the eyes of those hoping to see God's love, the light and warmth of it goes unshared.

Love *created* us. It's why we're here and what we're here to be, to show, and to reflect. If we miss the chance to follow in the footsteps of Jesus by walking in love, the flood of living light on our path will dim. Sometimes we're tempted to think we have to be involved in big movements, highly visible acts of charity, or every community volunteer project to feel like we're living a giving, loving, purposeful life. It's far simpler than that. God put us on the path of our purpose. We're exactly where we need to be, and we're a part of the lives we're here to touch. We have a divine role to play in each one of them.

A simple, quiet life is as powerful and purposeful as any other. Small kindnesses can leave the greatest impact. Humble acts of love can lead to an eternal decision. There is *no* insignificant measure of love in this world. Let's be quick to see where we can be a living light in every possible, loving way today.

Dear God,

My life is in Your hands, and my greatest purpose for living is love. Give me a quiet, listening heart today, so I don't miss a chance to be the light someone needs to see.

The Great Simplifier

With His love, He will calm all your fears.
ZEPHANIAH 3:17 NLT

Our lives would be simplified if we believed with all our hearts we had *nothing* to fear. The conversations we knew we had to have . . . the test results we were waiting to hear . . . the bills we didn't yet have the resources to pay—everything we fear works against the hope of living a simple life. For each fear that creeps in and threatens to steal our peace, there's a calming force to meet and defeat it. God's love is the most proactive power in our lives. It's trustworthy. It's *always* for us and working *constantly* for our good.

The hardest times to hold on to the security of God's love are when the conversations don't go well, the diagnoses aren't good, and the due dates don't get met. In these moments simplicity seems elusive if not impossible. We have to determine to hold on to truth with a firmer grip than ever because *nothing* is impossible with God. When things don't go according to plan or align with what we're hoping for, we have to *refuse* to let go of God's calming, courageous, and constant love.

It sounds trite on our most difficult days, but in the end love *always* wins. The conversation that went awry will lead to the right outcome eventually. The test result we didn't want to hear will result in our hearing the voice of God and experiencing the love of God in ways that will change us forever. The financial need met later than hoped will deepen our hope in God, knowing that He knew what we gained by trusting was worth far more than the cost of a late fee. His provision is faithful and more than enough.

God wants us to learn a simple life of *trust*. When we do, we allow Him to work through us as He planned. His is the best plan, to reveal our best selves, in order to reflect the best of Him in this world. Love is the great simplifier. If we believe He loves us more than anything else in the universe (and He *does*), we can live with the security, calm, and ease of a child in the arms of a perfect Father (which He *is*).

Dear God,
Calm my fears with Your love and presence
today, and build my brave trust in You.

Saturating Our Souls with Love

Thank God! . . . He uses us to spread the
knowledge of Christ everywhere,
like a sweet perfume.

II CORINTHIANS 2:14 NLT

When we've been around a campfire, it's hard to deny we were. The smell permeates our hair and everything we wear! It's a smell associated with simple, good things. We think of time with family and friends, camping, relaxing, taking a break from the busyness of life, and a little window of time to do nothing. Making time for it can feel like *everything* to our weary souls.

When the light of God is in us, the things we do saturate the people around us with His love. They remember they've been in our presence because we've been in *His*. Love can become a beautiful habit. The more we understand how deeply God loves us, the more His life-changing love will beam from our lives, leaving light in our wake. A heart in love with God is reflected in acts of love *for* God.

It can sound like a simple thing to know how much God loves us. But too often we forget how perfectly we're loved. Through all the mistakes we make and the mountains we face, God's love never wavers. By putting our mistakes on replay or allowing the mountain to overcome us with fear, the love holding us loses its place. God's love is our security. God's love is our hope. Being sure of it is the only way to live our lives in the simplest way: *love God most so we can love others best.*

When the day starts, start reclaiming your thoughts. If the mental tape recorder reminds you of what went wrong yesterday, turn it off. Play this instead: "I've never quit loving you and never will. Expect love, love, and more love!" (Jeremiah 31:3 *The Message*). Absolutely *nothing* can make God stop loving you. It simply *cannot* happen! Keep knowing it. Keep believing it. Keep it so ingrained in your mind and heart that love becomes the only thing guiding your actions. It's the best way to have the best days—and the only way to saturate the world with the sweet scent of God's never-ending love.

Dear God,

Your love for me is deeper, wider, and truer than I can fathom. Fill my mind and heart with reminders of it today so everyone around me feels it too.

Simply Being You

If you're content to simply be yourself,
your life will count for plenty.
MATTHEW 23:12 *THE MESSAGE*

Comparison is a great temptation and a terrible liar. It's too easy to see people's lives through a social media lens and assume they're more blessed, together, successful, or significant than we are. On the contrary, we might know someone who lives sacrificially and selflessly in every way yet doesn't feel their life is worth as much as the one getting all the accolades and attention. Neither rings true. There are no perfect lives, no matter how it looks in a post put up in the middle of their pain, their struggle, and their difficult days. None of us are exempt from suffering in this life. And no life, no matter how quietly it is lived, is worth less than any other.

We have to be on constant guard against comparison. The truth is, if we learn contentment in simply being who God created us to be, we'll know confidently that we're where we're supposed to be, doing exactly what we're meant to do. Every life is equally valuable. Every person is marvelously made. *Every* one of us is significantly loved by our heavenly Father. *God has no favorites.*

Whatever the day holds, know you're an invaluable part of God's plan. A simple life has all the meaning of one lived on a stage. Your life counts. You matter. If you walk to your neighbors to say hello and check on their well-being, it's no less important than giving a speech in front of thousands. Our paths are different, but our purpose is *priceless*. Greet today with confidence, see yourself as the individual, irreplaceable soul that you are, and know that each moment means something—because no one else in the world is YOU.

Dear God,

Thank You for creating me to be *me* and for opening my eyes to the value of my purpose. All that You have for me to do today is an all-important part of Your plan.

Living Lightly

You have been chosen by God Himself . . . so that you may show to others how God called you out of the darkness into His wonderful light.

1 PETER 2:9 TLB

The greatest way to be a light, the way to be a brighter light, and the way to attract more people to the source of light within us is to *live lightly*! Who are the people in your life that exude joy? Who are the people that inspire you to be more carefree? They probably have something in common. They've learned to let God carry the weight of their worry, doubt, and fear. They've resolved to *live lightly* in His promise to be everything, *always*. It's a hard-fought place for any of us to get to. But it's worth staying the course to get there. We are happiest when we're leaning on Him and shining brightest!

God chose you. There's a place in His purpose for you that's as unique as the gifts you've been given. No one else can light up a room the way you do! God mapped out the lives your life would shine into when He called you into His wonderful light. Each one of us is created for the steps we take, the path we follow, and the people we encounter. Nothing is by accident and no one we meet is a random engagement. God is in us, which means He's in every breath we take.

Love and light are companions of His presence. We have the privilege of bringing them into a world that needs their warmth more than ever. In distinct, personal ways God uses us to reach those who are searching for a glimpse of sunshine in their storm. God sees their hearts and knows their needs. He knows the words that will heal them, the actions that are most loving, and the kindnesses that will turn their hope toward Him. The wonderful light we walk in lets us live joyful, carefree lives. By living lightly, loving freely, and listening closely, we can be just where we're meant to be—and just what others need to see.

Dear God,

Fill me with the light of Your presence and the joy that's in it. Let my life be warm, inspiring, and a confident picture of Your constant care.

Moving Toward a Quiet Trust

Teach me, and I will be quiet;
show me where I have been wrong.

JOB 6:24 NIV

It's hard to learn anything if we go through our days at a breakneck pace. Yet God created us to learn—how to love better, how to trust more, how to know our value, how to let go of the controls and hold on to Him. We're here to realize how miraculously we're made and to discover that a simple life is anchored in a simple truth. God loves us too much to let us go. *Ever.* It doesn't matter if we get it all wrong some days. When we rush past opportunities to listen, to rest, to pray, to stop and get directions, there's a good chance we'll get a whole bunch of things wrong. But grace is patient, certain, and steadying.

Every day is another chance to move toward a simple life while pushing away from the chaos. When we get entangled in the idea that we have to accomplish a set number of tasks or prove our worth by the world's measure of success, we risk never being able to slow down and learn how to simply be quiet. It's a discipline we'll master only by asking for God's help. He sees the things we can't see. He's written our days. He wants us to remember how sufficient

He is and how infinitely He cares. It's up to us to quiet the noisy demands in our heads, the loud expectations we've put on ourselves, and the nagging impossibility of perfection—in our homes, our jobs, our families, and our social media posts.

Maybe we can start our days in a different way. Our eyes open with a quiet *thank You*. Our first deep breath brings a quiet smile. A healthy stretch from head to toe releases our hours into God's hands. There is nothing more comforting or faithful than His care. It's as relentless as our list of things to do, but He can be trusted with what gets done—and what doesn't. Remember the moments that make up the minutes belong to the One who's teaching us to simply *trust*.

Dear God,
Quiet my heart to hear Your voice, learn to trust,
and let go of the pressures controlling my day.
I give it all to You and the peace of Your care.

The Light of Hope and Restoration

*You're here to be light, bringing out
the God-colors in the world.*

MATTHEW 5:16 *THE MESSAGE*

When we want to add different, vibrant colors to a campfire, there are products we can buy to make it happen. The usual bright orange and yellow hues are there, along with shades of blue, green, and purple. The campfire becomes exciting to watch and holds our attention even more than it would normally. A single source of heat and light creates a captivating display of beauty.

The light of God is seen a little differently through each of our lives. Not a single person formed by His hand is exactly the same. Our one-of-a-kind personalities create a unique hue. And we have *every* reason to draw as much attention to who God is, as brightly, boldly, and as often as we can while we're in this world. Our unique gifts and traits are what make the light of God brilliant and beautiful to those around us. We should never want our light to be subdued or hidden. We're all created to shine forth the goodness of who He is. We're alive to bring His love to life with compassion, generosity, kindness, and joy.

If there was ever a time to put more love in our days, it's now. Even through the most difficult and dark seasons, God is the light that brings restoration and hope. We get to be His kindling! He'll work through us to rekindle the flames of community, and His light will burn brighter than we thought possible. We'll need to be paying attention to every open door and opportunity. God will look for lives ready to illuminate the world with love, and we'll become the attention-getters in the best ways, for the greatest good.

Dear God,
In every trial, Your light is our way through.
Show me what I can do to bring hope,
healing, and love where it's needed most.

Take your everyday, ordinary life—your sleeping, eating, going-to-work, and walking-around life—and place it before God as an offering. Embracing what God does for you is the best thing you can do for Him.

ROMANS 12:1 *THE MESSAGE*

A Simple Life of Letting Go

*There's an opportune time to do things, a right
time for everything on the earth . . . a right
time to hold on and another to let go.*

ECCLESIASTES 3:1, 6 *THE MESSAGE*

If we were asked to make a top ten list of obstacles standing in the way of living a simple life, what might the list look like? Maybe some of the obstacles would be the lack of solitude, a stressful job, unorganized spaces, too little time to spend with the people we love, or too many demands on our lives we don't think we can change. Our lists would vary, but a deeply ingrained mindset would probably find a way into them all. We just want to believe we're *doing* enough. We just want to feel we *are* enough.

A lot of us think that living a simpler life is, well, not simple at all. We have to stay driven. We must be ambitious. We need to set higher goals, influence more people, and work longer hours. There's another way to think about life. It's true, peaceful, good, and *simple*.

Quiet down before God, be prayerful before Him. Don't bother with those who climb the ladder, who elbow their way to the top (Psalm 37:7 *The Message*).

It is senseless for you to work so hard from early morning until late at night, fearing you will starve to death; for God wants His loved ones to get their proper rest (Psalm 127:2 TLB).

"Come to Me and I will give you rest—all of you who work so hard beneath a heavy yoke. Wear My yoke—for it fits perfectly—and let Me teach you; for I am gentle and humble, and you shall find rest for your souls; for I give you only light burdens" (Matthew 11:28 TLB).

If we aren't absolutely convinced of God's unconditional love for us, a simple life will continue to elude us. Overcoming the obstacles we know are complicating our days begins with knowing we're loved, valued, cared for, and held in the palm of God's hand. Absolutely *nothing* can keep Him from meeting every need in our lives—without an ounce of striving on our part.

Dear God,

Give me courage to simplify my life. Teach me how to slow down, rest when I need to, and trust completely in Your all-sufficient love.

The Only Thing Left Standing

Because He bends down and listens,
I will pray as long as I breathe!

PSALM 116:2 TLB

Have you ever bent down to listen to a child? There's something simple and beautiful about it. It lets them know you're truly hearing what they say. It makes them feel special. It gives them a sense of value and importance. They know you're taking the time to *focus on them*. Isn't it amazing to know God does that every time we speak to Him? What a simple gesture that carries a powerful message.

God listens. Every breath we take is one He gives with purpose and love. We're valued and we're important to Him. His focus is on us because the light of His love is *in* us, and it's what the world needs to become a brighter, better, more beautiful place. God made it simple. We're the complicators! If we pare down our lives to what matters most, what we can't live without, and what God created us for, love is the only thing left standing. "Trust steadily in God, hope unswervingly, love extravagantly. And the best of the three is love" (I Corinthians 13:13 *The Message*).

How can we make today all about love? Can we be better listeners? Can we spread a little hope through a smile, an encouraging word, a handwritten note, or a quick text? If we're having a day where we simply need rest and direction, God is bending down to listen to us. If we're the ones who need to feel loved, God is reaching out to hold us. He never asks us to give away what He doesn't give to us in abundance. Love is who He is, and we are first *His*.

Dear God,

My heart is thankful for Your heart—the heart of a Father. Knowing I'm perfectly loved makes me a brighter light in the world, created to shine with the beauty of You.

The Love in the Chase

Your beauty and love chase after me every day of my life.
PSALM 23:6 THE MESSAGE

When the flames of a bonfire chase the darkness of night away, an area that was once pitch black lights up like the middle of day. And all kinds of *good things* can be seen. The comfort of community. Friends laughing. Kids playing. Families together. It's a good thing for God to see too, because He created us for one another. Light has a way of revealing love, and maybe that's the way it's supposed to be.

Love is the reason the Light of the world came to save us. It's the light that shatters *every* darkness in our lives. Fear. Shame. Doubt. Hopelessness. None of it can overcome the love of God. When we let His light and love shine through our lives, a lot of good things come into view. We see the best in people and believe the best about them. We see our compassion grow stronger and our patience grow longer. We see the hope in them searching for the kindness in us—where they'll find the goodness in Him.

What would happen if we woke up each morning thinking about the beauty and love of God chasing us? It's never going to give up! It's going to keep chasing us until it overtakes *every* doubt we have that we're infinitely valued, completely forgiven, and eternally loved. We are God's prized creation. Our lives are a reflection of His beauty. Loving our path is praising His work, and it's altogether praiseworthy. Let's face the day believing that if we shed light on the love of God surrounding us, it will reveal only good things—because that's what our *always good God* gives.

Dear God,

Help my heart see the good in every part
of You, everything You allow, and every
course You set for my life. Let my doubt
be extinguished by Your light and love.

The Comfort of a Carefree Life

Live carefree before God; He is most careful with you.

I PETER 5:7 THE MESSAGE

Living carefree and living a simple life are synonymous. There are many things we care *about*, but there shouldn't be anything we don't trust God to take care *of*. This doesn't mean we sit around and do nothing. It means we don't pace the floor, stress out, and lose sleep worrying about everything God has promised to provide. We have a lot of the same needs that other people have in this world, and God meets them in different ways through different people. He *knows* us. He's *careful* with us. He cares about our spiritual growth as much as our physical needs. *Everything* in our lives is on His radar and in His care.

His love truly is in the details. We should always be looking for it. If we paid attention to the things He does the way He pays attention to our needs, we'd see Him *everywhere*. Our hearts would find gratefulness in the recognition. Our minds would find peace in His presence. Our spirits would find a renewed hope to carry us a little further on our journey. It's comforting to simply read the words *God is careful with you.*

Life isn't always careful with us. People aren't always careful with us. Sometimes we're not careful with ourselves. We're slow to forgive our mistakes, merciless when it comes to our weaknesses, and forgetful about the depth of God's love for us. A simple, carefree life is ours by grace. We should grab it with both hands! It covers, comforts, and carries us. It forgives, follows, and frees us. *God is most careful with you. Grace is most generous with you.* Those are good thoughts to put on replay today.

Dear God,

Help me be mindful of Your love. Remind me to be kind to myself. Give me the strength of Your joy and the peace of Your sufficient grace, no matter what the day brings.

Waiting Quietly

Let all that I am wait quietly before
God, for my hope is in Him.

PSALM 62:5 NLT

Getting quiet around a campfire comes naturally. The setting lends itself to quiet reflection while we watch the flames dance and feel the warmth on our feet. Conversations get loud and then lull as everyone sits back to just enjoy being together. It's the simple moments that end up making the sweetest memories.

Our hearts are more in tune with God when we sit quietly. He doesn't get the chance to connect with us in the clamor of our busy days because we don't take the time to listen. It feels like we don't *have* the time to listen. Too many days feel like we're trying to squeeze thirty-six hours of to-dos into the twenty-four hours we're given. Our sleep suffers and our minds never stop churning.

Making a deliberate effort to slow down is well worth the reward. When we let *all* that we are "wait quietly before God," we get all the benefits. Peace has a chance to settle in. Gratefulness comes to the surface, and hope emerges with it. Things that were drowning out God's voice in our hearts and minds sink steadily out of sight. The stormy waters go calm. This is how we find the energy to face our busy days without getting burned out and overwhelmed. We have to give quiet the time it needs so God can give us what *we* need.

What can we let wait today while we take some time to wait quietly before God? Our sense of urgency to get a certain number of things done is often self-induced. Learning to relax our expectations and the demands we put on ourselves can free up our time *and* our minds. It can create the quiet spaces we need to think about good things. To be grateful. To breathe deeper. To savor calmness. To listen to the words God wants us to hear clearest and most: "I will be your God throughout your lifetime . . . I made you, and I will care for you" (Isaiah 46:4 NLT).

Dear God,

Show me where I can slow down the pace
of my day and sit quietly with You. My
strength and hope are in You alone.

A Simple, Secure, and Surrendered Life

I've learned by now to be quite content
whatever my circumstances.

PHILIPPIANS 4:12 *THE MESSAGE*

A simple life is not something we arrive at one day by coincidence. It's the result of a choice or a change of circumstance. There are things that happen in our lives that move us in the direction of living lighter and being content with less. Moving into a new home brings an opportunity to purge things we haven't seen, or used, for years. Loss of a job leads us to a place of learning to live without things we'd grown used to having. What our ever-changing circumstances teach us, if we're willing to lean into God's care, is that contentment is a *gift*. And a simple life is far more satisfying than we expect.

God's ways are never complicated, and our lives are *least* complicated when we trust Him to know what we need and give what we need. It's as simple as that. The path of our spiritual growth is clear to God. We can't see what He has planned for us, so we can't know exactly what it's going to take to prepare us for it. God is most interested in drawing us closer to Him and least interested in our remaining spiritually stagnant. Growth can be hard and painful. But it's the key to a simple, secure, and surrendered life of trust in our unfailing Father.

The path can feel incredibly long at times. In a world where we're used to getting a lot of things on a fast track, our patience is out of shape for lack of exercise. But time teaches. God's wisdom prevails. He wastes nothing—not a single minute—of the journey He knows will lead us to the place of our highest purpose. It's going to be good. It's going to be a gift. It's going to give us a contentment deeper than we imagined was possible.

Dear God,

Your timing is not mine, but I trust the steps of my journey to You. When I get impatient or discouraged, give me peace and renew my hope. I know Your love will always do what's best for me.

Love Ignites the Light

I have come as a Light to shine in this dark
world, so that all who put their trust in Me
will no longer wander in the darkness.

JOHN 12:46 TLB

It's amazing how light in any amount pierces the darkness. It can be a match, a candle, a campfire, or a bonfire, and the darkness doesn't stand a chance against it. When we spend our lives being a light, whether in kindnesses we scatter every day or charities we build across the globe, we're doing more than we realize to brighten this dark world. A candle can be seen with the naked eye from over a mile away. We can *never* compare the light we share. It all matters. It all makes an eternal difference. Love ignites the light in us—and God's love is the most powerful, life-changing force on this earth.

When we feel pressured to do more, be more, or accomplish more, we have to go back to the love that created us. Each one of us is designed to play an equally important role in the moving parts of this world. When we start to think our day-to-day doesn't matter, especially in the rut of a routine, we forget how infinitely valuable we are. When we don't think our light is making enough of an impact, we dismiss the place and purpose God chose for us. *We are right where we're meant to be, shining directly into the lives that need us.*

It's challenging to stay the course if we see ourselves doing more, but God's timing is not our timing. Dreams don't have an expiration date. If we believe our days are written in perfect order (*they are*) by the God who authored the desires of our hearts (*He did*), we can be the light we're called to be—right now, right here, and in the lives right in front of us.

Dear God,

Let me be Your light and love today
without interruption, serving You with
a thankful heart and a joyful spirit.

What Comes with the Sun

O Lord, You are my light! You make my darkness bright.

II SAMUEL 22:29 TLB

Light draws attention. Love brings warmth. In us, they work together to point to their source. Our lives are like transmitters that bring God's light and love into the world—to those we meet, to the people in our lives, and to the family we're given. Being human, we're not going to get it right all the time. There will be some short-circuiting in the transmission because we're imperfect. We'll lose our tempers, say harsh words, act selfishly, and sometimes feel like giving up. God understands. His compassion for us in our weaknesses and failures led to the grace that covers us. Because of His incredible love we have a clean slate and a new start every morning.

When we have dark days, there are simple ways to brighten them. A bouquet of flowers, fresh air, our favorite comfort food, a funny movie, or a good book can lighten the heaviness. To be a steady reflection of God's light and love, we have to stay aware of how He wired us. What makes us feel alive and energetic? What makes us smile and feel a deep-down thankfulness for the grace we're given? We get recharged when we identify and *do* those things. We're better at showing God's love to others when we take time to bask in a few restorative, simple joys. They're all connected to the way God knit us together, and it's good to go back to them when we can.

Today we might feel like jumping out of bed, or we might want to pull the blankets over our heads, hoping the daylight and the demands that come with it disappear. But demands aren't all that come with the sunrise. Fathomless love comes with it. Endless compassion comes with it. Grace for the day comes with it. And God is *in it*—bringing all the strength you're going to need.

Dear God,

Thank You for the unique way I'm wired

and the simple joys You give that restore

my soul. I see Your love in each one.

A Crash Course in Simple Living

In all you do, I want you to be free from worry.

I CORINTHIANS 7:32 TLB

A spur-of-the-moment weekend camping trip is a healthy crash course in finding out how little we need to live simply, freely, and sufficiently. There's no time to overthink or overpack. Hot dogs and marshmallows, check. Blankets, check. Firewood, check. What we forget, we manage without. It's one of the greatest bonding opportunities for families or solo adventurers who want to spend time with God. It's our chance to get away from the usual noise of our lives and get in tune with the world God created.

The campfire is one of the most vital parts of the experience. We can go without a lot of things in the middle of nowhere, but we need light and heat if we want to see, cook, and stay warm at night. It's also one of the best parts of the venture. A campfire is the comforting center of attention when night falls. It's the gathering place. It somehow burns away the pressures of the daily grind and the stress that goes with it. It inspires us to think about how to simplify other areas of our lives, because getting back to the bare basics does something inexplicably soothing to our souls.

Freeing our lives from worry requires some getting away now and then. We have to be reminded that the simple things bring the most satisfying rewards. The physical comforts and luxuries we've grown used to every day are crowding out the deeper needs within us. If we never quietly connect with the God who loves us most and the people we love spending our lives with, we miss the greatest reasons to be alive. Stress, worry, overworking, and never slowing down will eventually suffocate the life God wants for us—a life free from worry and full of peace, joy, and love.

Dear God,

I want to live a life with less worry and more of You. Help me make the time and take the time to grow closer to You and the people I love.

Simply Sitting Still

In quietness and confidence is your strength.

ISAIAH 30:15 NLT

Try to think of one or two simple activities that are as relaxing and quieting as sitting around a campfire. For most of us, being fireside is in the top five. There's something special about simply being *still*—on a beach, in a coffee shop, or on our front porch. Wherever we are and however we can, stillness inspires us to quiet our minds, relax, reflect, and pray. *It's always a good thing.*

God loves it when we stop moving and savor the hours. Life is a gift that's underappreciated in the constant rush of our days. In Psalm 102:3 the psalmist writes, "My days disappear like smoke" (NLT). We can all relate to his observation. The only way to be more deliberate about living each day to the fullest is by making decisions that leave room for simply sitting still. *In quietness and confidence is your strength.* These are God's words. They're a reminder that the way to a life of fulfillment is through Him. It comes by getting quiet, remaining confident, and waiting patiently for His perfect timing in all things. Clamoring around to find what we need in any other way will only weaken our trust muscles and lead to a shallow, fearful life that falls far short of the abundant one He has for us.

The habit of stillness can start slowly and in small ways. Five minutes carved out of an afternoon to walk outside and just sit, breathe, and stay quiet. Doing the same thing at night under a canopy of stars will do wonders to quiet our souls. Even sitting at our favorite window in the house for a few minutes to feel the sun on our face and look at the sky. Creation is saturated with God. *The earth is filled with His glory.* He'd love for you to take time to quiet your mind and be confident in His care today. He has *everything* in your life under control—and He plans to fill it with good things.

Dear God,

You see every pressure I'm under,

every care I'm tempted to carry,

and every demand tugging at me today.

Remind me often that my strength is in

You alone and the confidence I can put

in Your constant, compassionate care.

The tendency of fire is to go out; watch the fire on the altar of your heart. Anyone who has tended a fireplace knows that it needs to be stirred up occasionally.

WILLIAM BOOTH

The Enemy of Simplicity

*He knows all hidden things, for He is light,
and darkness is no obstacle to Him.*

DANIEL 2:22 TLB

There isn't anything in our lives or any part of who we are that is hidden from God. Knowing that He sees all our imperfections, mistakes, and thoughts and yet loves us unconditionally and *unflinchingly* is astounding. What Jesus did to prove that love is beyond astounding! That's our worth in God's eyes. It can't be measured. And we couldn't create an obstacle to keep His light and love from reaching us if we tried. Some days it feels like we're throwing out one hurdle after another to test it. We fear what we can't control, we stress what we can't change, we ignore what we know to be true, and we wear ourselves out in the process.

We were made to live simple lives, physically and spiritually. God loves us. God has us. If there's one word He'd like to shout from the heavens, it would probably be *RELAX*! Too much is the enemy of simplicity. Too much to do. Too much to prove. Too much to attain. Too much fear. Too much comparison, complaining, and trying to control our lives. God wants to help us reach a simpler life with two words: *TRUST ME.* Oh, how free we would be if we believed without a doubt that we live, move, and have our being in Him!

We can start right now. We can grip the handle of hope when our trust is under assault. We can pray without ceasing when fear tries to enfold us. We can remove the expectations we put on ourselves and those guided by the world's standard or opinion. And even on the toughest days, we can go back to the deepest truth: "My spirit may grow weak, but God remains the strength of my heart; He is mine forever" (Psalm 73:26 NLT).

Dear God,

Reveal every part of me and every area of

my life that needs to be simplified. Restore

my childlike trust in You and give me

courage to let go of anything that keeps

me from giving everything to You.

Calmness in Contrast

Calmness can lay great offenses to rest.

ECCLESIASTES 10:4 NIV

There's no question that the entire world could use some collective calmness right now. It's difficult for any of us to stay even-keeled in our daily lives if we spend even a fraction of our time reading headlines or listening to the news. Living a quiet, simple life feels like more of a battle than ever before, but God has never asked us to fight a battle on our own. We've always needed Him and we always will.

How do we get to a state of calmness, to a place unaffected by the harshness of the world around us? We begin by turning our focus to the little things. The *simple*, little things. Instead of staring at the television, we try a new recipe. When we're tempted to sit and scroll, we sit and read a book we've been wanting to start. It takes a second to redirect our thoughts and make a better choice—a quieter choice, a choice that will make our lives begin to feel simpler and more grounded. Calmness is a state we can master with the help of God's ever-present Spirit. It's not as impossible as it might seem. And if there's any hope of dialing back the screen time, the noise, and the negativity, inside our homes is the best place to do it.

When our lives display a calmness that stands in contrast to the world's chaos, the light of God shines a little brighter from it. Love's reflection is a little clearer in it. God's goodness flows a little easier through it. We can follow our hearts in the calm and the quiet—and maybe little by little our simple change of choices can start to change the world.

Dear God,

My days bring countless choices. Quiet my heart so I can follow Yours. Give me wisdom to choose well and the strength to follow through. In calmness there is peace, and that's what I want my life to reflect.

The Only Way to a Simpler Way

When I sit in darkness, the Lord Himself will be my Light.

MICAH 7:8 TLB

There are days when it feels like the walls are closing in. Too many things have gone wrong and overshadowed the things we hoped would go right. Our hearts are broken, our fears are growing, and all we can see is a narrowing path forward that's barely lit. But forward is the way we'll go! Love's pure light will start to glow. The Lord will step in, where we sit, and flood the path once dimly lit. Sometimes a simple rhyme can be the lighthearted reminder we need that God will *never* leave us alone and *never* let us down! *So let's not stay down.*

Disappointments are not the end of our story, and they're not the prevalent theme. God is about restoration. God sees the outcome of the downward turns in our lives, and His plan is in place to change their course. We might not see it right now, but He sees it. More beautifully, He sees the *very good things* coming on the other side of the dark patches. They're good things that will fortify our trust and make us a lot stronger for the next challenge we face.

The only way to a simpler way of life is letting God have His way! "If you want favor with both God and man, and a reputation for good judgment and common sense, then trust the Lord completely; don't ever trust yourself. In everything you do, put God first, and He will direct you and crown your efforts with success" (Proverbs 3:5–6 TLB). Loving God most means putting Him first. It's great wisdom to follow because it takes all the pressure off us and puts it in the lap of the One who loves *us* most. When our emotions go up and down like a teeter-totter, His don't change. He's involved in our lives constantly, purposefully, and lovingly—and we can trust Him as fully in the dark as we do in the light.

Dear God,

You are my way today! In all things I'll trust

You, with all my heart I'll love You, and for

all the good things ahead I praise You!

Simplifying for Our Sanity

Commit everything you do to the Lord.
Trust Him to help you do it, and He will.

PSALM 37:5 TLB

elieving we're loved as we are and knowing there isn't a
need too insignificant for God to notice or one too big
for Him to meet is not an easy task. We're doers. We like
to stay busy thinking about how we're going to get things
done. We make lists and plans. We set short- and long-term
goals. We read books on how to stay motivated, how to
master our destiny, and how to make a greater impact with
our lives.

How in the world do we get to a simple life through all
the lists, plans, goals, expectations, and advice? The world
we live in is relentless about distracting us from the life God
created us to enjoy. Our lives were never meant to draw us
away from Him. If we stand a chance of standing down the
madness, it has to start with committing *everything* we do
to Him. We have to change the *how-tos* that we *go to*:

*"You are right and You do right, God; Your decisions are
right on target. You rightly instruct us in how to live ever
faithful to You (Psalm 119:137 The Message).*

"Are you tired? Worn out? . . . Come to Me. Get away with Me and you'll recover your life. I'll show you how to take a real rest" (Matthew 11:28 *The Message*).

God is not against us reaching our goals and realizing our dreams. He's the One who planted those desires in our hearts to begin with. But when our ambitions take the driver's seat and we lose the joy that gives us strength, it's time to ask for the wisdom to get back to a simpler life. One where the simple things we enjoy with the people we love make it to the top of our priority list—and we trust God to help us *keep* them there.

Dear God,

I surrender my busy life to Your guidance, wisdom, and will. Let everything I do be balanced by Your design and directed by Your hand so I can love the people in my life the way You love me.

Let God Have It All

*Choose to love the Lord your God and
to obey Him and to cling to Him,
for He is your life and the length of your days.*

DEUTERONOMY 30:20 TLB

We don't have to reach a certain age to have a clearer perspective about the best way to live simpler, more meaningful lives. Centenarians are often interviewed for their secrets to longevity. There are some common denominators: regular exercise, time to de-stress, being part of a community (often a religious one), and commitment to family.

We can start practicing one of those right now. "Let Him have all your worries and cares, for He is always thinking about you and watching everything that concerns you" (I Peter 5:7 TLB). If we can fine-tune our thought life every day to the Word of God, we can live with more joy than we ever thought possible. Joy is strength. A cheerful heart is good medicine. Laughter has been referred to as "internal aerobics."

Joy is not a feeling; it's a *force*. It's powerful and palpable. It's contagious and *courageous*. It's living proof to a dark world that we have a loving, kind, and faithful Father who has our back and every single one of our burdens. The more joy we cultivate in our lives, the stronger we become and the brighter we shine.

Live lightly today and be a light to others. Give God the glory and the gratefulness for the gift of another day to love on our people, help in our community, and enjoy the simple moments. They're passing quickly, but not without meaning when we pay attention and appreciate each one. The love that has no end has *us*, and when we put our trust in it, everything falls perfectly into place.

Dear God,

You are my life and the light that leads me
through my days. I want to rest in Your
perfect love and make the most of my
moments for Your glory and Your purpose.

Simple Things for the Smile

Oh, put God to the test and see how kind
He is! See for yourself the way His mercies
shower down on all who trust in Him.

PSALM 34:8 TLB

Let's make today a shower of simple things. Whatever little things we enjoy doing, let's find a way to squeeze in as many as we can. We're going to look for all the kindnesses God puts in our day, too, the ones we normally don't notice because we're not paying attention. Maybe there will be a pink morning sky, cotton candy–colored clouds, and a bright orange sun that make us feel incredibly grateful for the newness, forgiveness, and warmth the day brings. It's all God, and it's every bit *good*.

If lunch is normally a time to work or hurry through, take time to sit somewhere away from the phone calls, emails, noise, and obligations. Maybe indulge in something you love but usually resist, like french fries or an ice-cream cone. Treat yourself to afternoon tea if you love the tiny, relaxing spot of peace in your day. Make a little plate of snacks just for you, and just because.

We can't keep rushing past the little things we love doing. We can't keep racing through our lives forgetting to appreciate the simple things that bring us joy. We don't all love the same things, but that's really the most *beautiful* thing. We're marvelously and *uniquely* made. It's the amazing stamp of pricelessness God puts on our lives. When we do what we love, no matter what it takes, no matter what we have to let go for a few minutes, no matter when or how we make it happen, we're thanking God for *who we are*. He loves us and loves seeing us savor the little joys in life that make us smile. He knew what they were before we did, and He's *absolutely* smiling with us.

Dear God,

Show me how to slow down. Remind me that Your love is in the little things, the big things, and *all* things throughout my day. When I see and appreciate them, I see and appreciate *You*.

The Light Is On!

You have turned on my light! The Lord my
God has made my darkness turn to light.

PSALM 18:28 TLB

Just as the shades of blue, green, orange, and yellow blend together to bring beauty and vibrancy to a campfire, our lives blend together to bring beauty and vibrancy to the world. We have unique gifts. We're given individual purposes. We walk different paths.

God is the light in each one of us, but we're in control of the dimmer switch. We choose how brightly we shine by choosing how we live our lives. God made it surprisingly simple: *Love Me and love others. Don't worry about who to love; I'll bring them into your life. Don't overthink how to love them; it's often just a simple smile, opening a door, a kind word, or a thoughtful gesture. Don't be offended if they don't respond in a loving way; they won't forget the light they saw in you because it comes from Me. I see their heart.*

"It started when God said, 'Light up the darkness!' and our lives filled up with light as we saw and understood God in the face of Christ, all bright and beautiful" (II Corinthians 4:6 The Message). We didn't even start the light that burns in us. It's *from* God and it's *for* God. Love is the oxygen that keeps it going. We're here to supply it in a consistent, coura-geous, and compassionate way. It's the only thing that's go-ing to make anything better in this world. Love, love, love, and never give up—that's a purpose deposited in each one of us. Our special gifts can blend together to light the whole earth if we determine to love well and love always.

God is our reason to do it. God is our strength to accom-plish it. God is our hope to burn brighter than ever before. And today is another chance to let our light shine!

Dear God,

Thank You for the light in me and the love

that keeps it burning. Use me to bring change

to my corner of the world, in the lives around

me, through the ways You reveal today.

Striking a Balance

Trust the Lord and sincerely worship Him;
think of all the tremendous things
He has done for you.
I SAMUEL 12:24 TLB

Humble is a synonym of *simple*, and it might be the best one to use when we think about defining a life that honors God. When we think of even a fraction of the tremendous things He's done for us personally and in the course of our lives, sincere gratitude and praise come easily. Trusting Him continually is a little more challenging.

In today's world, life can be pushy and loud. Work for more, sacrifice for better, put in the time to get the rewards, the accolades, and the impressive annual income. There's a truth whispering beneath it all:

"If God gives such attention to the appearance of wildflowers—most of which are never even seen—don't you think He'll attend to you, take pride in you, do His best for you? What I'm trying to do here is to get you to relax, to not be so preoccupied with getting, so you can respond to God's giving. People who don't know God and the way He works fuss over these things, but you know both God and how He works. Steep your life

in God-reality, God-initiative, God-provisions. Don't worry about missing out. You'll find all your everyday human concerns will be met" (Matthew 6:30–33 *The Message*).

Knowing our worth to God and steeping our lives in His love for us are the ways to trust that everything we'll ever need, He'll *always* provide. Believing Him at His word is how we strike a balance between working hard and working ourselves weary. It grieves Him to see us bound to the latter.

God is tremendously good. You have eternal value. Nothing is more important than living humbly before Him with a simple trust and a servant heart. God doesn't promote "striving"; He promotes a life of trust, humility, and purpose—and it's more fulfilling than anything.

Dear God,

Simply trusting You is the way I'll get to the life I long for. My needs are met by Your abundant love and faithfulness every day. Help me stay humble in Your truth.

His life is the
light that shines
through the
darkness—and
the darkness
can never
extinguish it.

JOHN 1:5 TLB

Simple Trust and the Turning Tide

Make it your ambition to lead a quiet life.

I THESSALONIANS 4:11 NIV

Most of us would probably describe our daily lives as anything but quiet. Whether we work in the home, from home, outside the home, or away from home, there's likely a degree of hectic that prevents us from defining our life as a quiet one. The race of our days might even inspire the occasional cry for help, or just a good cry.

There's no weakness in letting the tears flow. It's soul cleansing and stress relieving. Every one of our tears has God's attention. "You have seen me tossing and turning through the night. You have collected all my tears and preserved them in Your bottle! You have recorded every one in Your book" (Psalm 56:8 TLB). When God asks us to make it our ambition to live a quiet life, He doesn't mean it literally. The quietness He desires for our life is found in trusting Him. Simply *trusting Him*.

We need a quiet trust, deep down, that drowns out the noise of the lies in our heads saying, "You're not going to make it," "This is a mess even God won't clean up for you," or, "There's no way God's love can reach you here." Every ounce of our being has to trust that not *one* of those thoughts rings true. God loves you too much to author any thought that reflects anything but love or truth. Truth like this: "The very day I call for help, the tide of battle turns. . . . This one thing I know: God is for me! (Psalm 56:9 TLB).

God can be trusted completely. He's for you every hour of every day. It's time to be ambitious about living a quiet life. A life marked by quiet confidence in the face of any challenge. A life secure in truth. You will not be left alone, you will not be let down, and you will not be separated from the love that will *never* give up on you. Today can be trusted in the hands of your unfailing Father, and with Him controlling the tide of the battle, *nothing* is impossible.

Dear God,
I trust You. There's nothing that can
defeat me or pull me from the arms of love
carrying me. Give me the strength I need
to stand in Your favor and faithfulness.

All We Need to Remember

All you need to remember is that
God will never let you down.

I CORINTHIANS 10:13 *THE MESSAGE*

F ive little words for the reward of a simple life: *all you need to remember*. The love notes to us from God are countless, but memorizing enough of them will transform our thinking, squelch our insecurity, and simplify our days in the best ways. Here are a few to remember: *My love for you is constant. My love for you is infinite. My love for you is unfailing. My love for you is immovable. My love for you is forgiving, fueled by grace, and filled with kindness.* If we put that list in the forefront of our memory bank, we'll live the rest of our days realizing we're wealthier than we ever dreamed!

No matter how many times it's been said, sung, or hung on the walls of our homes, *love is all we need*. To know how perfectly loved we are in spite of our imperfections is truly all we need to live a simple, full life. When our hearts are filled with affirmations of God's love and the pressures of life knock us over, love spills out. When our minds are renewed every day by God's unfailing love and circumstances try to dim our light, love shines through. *All we need to re-*

member is how all-consuming God's love for us is and how powerful it is when it permeates every part of our being.

If God could weed out the things in our hearts and minds that weigh us down, He'd start with worry. He'd pull out all the negative thoughts and the lies He could *never* author. He'd dig up the doubts trying to take root, and He'd pluck out everything that isn't grounded in His love. Then He'd water all the good stuff with truth. And a simpler, happier life would start to take shape.

Let's make this our mind-renewing verse today: "Nothing can ever separate us from God's love" (Romans 8:38 NLT). *All we need to remember* is that today is going to be all kinds of good from the always-loving God who will *never* let us down!

Dear God,

Take everything from my heart and mind
that gets in the way of me remembering how
faithful, loving, and good You are every day.

Falling into the Stillness

Be still, and know that I am God!
PSALM 46:10 NLT

Have you ever been at a playground and watched a parent coaxing their child to let go of their grip on the monkey bars they're hanging from? The parent stands ready to catch them without fail, but to the child, holding on to the bar still feels more secure than letting go, no matter how much they trust Mom or Dad. No one likes to risk falling, even if they know a pair of loving arms is there to catch them.

When God tells us to be still, He's essentially telling us to *let go*. He's asking us to let go of the control-grip we have on our lives. He's asking us to pray about everything and wait patiently for the answers. He's asking us to release our lives into His loving arms, where we're always held safely and securely.

But sometimes we like to hold on to the solution we have to our problem a little longer, just in case we can do it without God's help. And we like to hang tight for a little while in our troubling circumstances to see if they shift, just in case we don't need to bother God with the details. Why is it hard for us to let go and let God be who He is? He's a loving Father who will *never* fail us. And when suffering does come, when days are difficult, when we need to feel loved and comforted, aren't His arms the best place to be?

Let's devote today to letting go. Let's revel in falling carelessly into the loving arms of God. It's going to feel great to relax our grip on everything that's trying to shake our trust and shatter our peace. We're going to be held close. We're going to be held steady. We're going to know without a doubt that we're wrapped in a love that will never change or loosen its grip on our lives—all while we're learning to *love* the lack of control.

Dear God,

Hold me in Your everlasting love and give me peace in knowing that letting go is the only way to let You have first place in my life.

Avoiding the Smoke

Then I observed all the work and ambition
motivated by envy. What a waste! Smoke.
And spitting into the wind.

ECCLESIASTES 4:4 *THE MESSAGE*

Have you ever felt like you're playing a version of musical chairs around a campfire to avoid the smoke? It usually ends up being a futile (but fun) attempt to dodge it completely. Once the fire really gets going and the smoke calms down, so does the need to keep running in circles!

Trying to compete or stay on the same level as everyone around us is a lot like running in circles. And wisdom warns us that it's never a good ambition to have. It's a great way to feel overwhelmed and unhappy, but those aren't good either. The best way to live well is to stay in the center of God's will. There'll never be anything there to drive us away or have us running in circles. It's there that we feel most connected to our purpose and secure in the love that lights our way. We'll see more clearly where we should go and what we should do.

The Spirit of God leads by *peace*. The guidance will always be in line with the truth of God's Word. If we ever feel like jumping out of our seats to move in a different direction, it's probably a good idea to sit back down and seek more wisdom. God gives it freely to those who ask. It's worth more than any material gain because it helps direct our steps to a life of true fulfillment and genuine joy. "For wisdom and truth will enter the very center of your being, filling your life with joy" (Proverbs 2:10 TLB). There's nothing simpler than asking God for what we need and knowing He'll give in the way He always does—*immeasurably more than we ask or imagine!*

Dear God,

I ask for wisdom to make simple, good, right choices in my life. As You lead by peace, I'll follow with gratefulness. Make my steps sure and my way clear today.

Every Hopeful Step of the Journey

*Let us run with patience the particular
race that God has set before us.*

HEBREWS 12:1 TLB

The difficult places in our lives will often push us in simpler directions. We reassess what's truly important. We discover how much we can live without and how much weight some things have that should be given a lot less of our energy. We start to notice the birds singing at first daylight, how good the sun feels on our faces, and how amazing it is to see flowers emerge from the frozen ground in early spring. They're God things calling for our attention. It's God reminding us we have His *full* attention, in the hope we start to notice again.

Life can feel like a race a lot of the time. But it doesn't have to be one we rush through and forget to enjoy. When we trust that God is with us every step of the way—that no matter what, everything will be *okay*—life takes on the pace it should. It's a more relaxed rhythm when we realize His ways are the best ways. Darkness, as terrifying as it can feel when we're in it, will not last and has no power to stay. The light is coming, and it's going to make things clear.

Times and circumstances bring sadness, suffering, and loss. But God *never* turns His back on our story. He cries with us in the sad parts, celebrates with us in the happy ones, and walks with us through every challenge. When we fall face down on the course without the strength or desire to pull ourselves back up, we learn we don't have to. God does the lifting and shows us how to *keep going*. Back on our feet we can *know* He's cheering, *Don't give up; live! Look for Me everywhere; I'm there.* You're not alone and you never will be. This journey isn't yours but *yours and God's*—and every breath of it is worth the life of the One who breathed His last for every brave and hopeful step you take.

Dear God,

Praise You for Your constant presence.

Thank You for the eternal hope You give.

Let me live with confidence in Your

faithfulness every day and stand

firmly in the power of Your love.

The Path to Peace and Quiet

Pray for all people. Ask God to help them . . .
so that we can live peaceful and quiet lives
marked by godliness and dignity.

1 TIMOTHY 2:1–2 NLT

Some days it can feel like we're moving further away from living peaceful, quiet lives with one another and closer to living in a world where too many are defensive and unforgiving. It's heartbreaking. It can leave us tired, weary, and wanting to curl up under a blanket until kindness and compassion come out again. But while we have the covers over our heads, we also have the incredible power to bring the change we long for. *We can pray for each other.*

As simple as it sounds, too much of the time we speed through our days without uttering a single prayer for our leaders, our friends, and those who need to see the love of God and the kindness of His heart. Being part of the solution is loving people bravely every day, no matter how deep our differences run. We have the chance to be light bearers in the darkness, love bringers in the heaviness, and prayer warriors in a battle-weary world.

Love in motion creates miracles all around us. Hearts are healed, encouraged, and *changed*. Hope is ignited. We begin to see a better world and a way to get there. There's a lot to do, but prayer, light, and love are the collective force that can do what it takes.

How can we start in a small, simple way to initiate a love chain reaction today? God has the plan if we have the persistence! The opportunities will land in front of us, inside or outside our homes, and we should take every one of them. When we do, we should pray for even more chances to love people and bring light into the world. It's the most beautiful way to bring the brightest change.

Dear God,

Let me be a light in the world

that overcomes darkness through

prayer, love, and hope.

Grace Is in It Minute by Minute

How kind He is! How good He is!
So merciful, this God of ours!

PSALM 116:5 TLB

The hope in a simple wildflower . . . the compassion in a colorful sunrise . . . the wonder in a starry sky . . . the kindness in a cloudless day—*so merciful, this God of ours!* Lord, don't let us miss all this! Our lives don't have to be busy to mean something. Days don't have to be scheduled from morning until night to be productive. We can stop and stare at Your goodness. We can simply take time for *You.*

God knows what each one of our days looks like. He knows what we're going to see, what we'll say, who will be in them, and how we'll react to what comes. His grace is in it minute by minute. We don't have to think about every detail of our day if we pray about it first. *Lord, I'm giving the day to You. I trust You with every part of it.* Inviting Him in takes the stress off us. Our minds will be freed up to follow His lead. His goodness will follow us. Demands on our time that don't get met will be easier to let go of, because we surrendered our plans to God's plan. His is always the best one.

Trusting God with our *whole* heart is an exhilarating, freeing feeling. It carries us to a place of confidence that nothing in this world is able to give us. It's joyful. And at the end of every day we don't have to go over a mental score sheet to see how we did. We'll rest in knowing God's already marked it *"well done"* with a smiley face. His is the only approval that matters. His is the heart that cares for us most and loves us best. Tomorrow will be waiting with its schedules, to-dos, and demands, but don't worry. God's already there, and He's ready to be trusted with whatever it holds.

Dear God,

I can trust You with all my days from start to finish. Give me strength to be the best I can be in them for Your purpose and glory.

No Need to Compete

Am I now trying to win the approval of human beings,
or of God? Or am I trying to please people? If I were still
trying to please people, I would not be a servant of Christ.
GALATIANS 1:10 NIV

It's relaxing to be around people who don't care about pleasing other people. It's such an admirable way to live, and it can't be a simple one to get to. Why do we get caught up in image and comparison? Is it because approval and admiration feel like love and acceptance? If so, it's the great deception. Love is the deepest desire of every heart, and it's the way God created us. That makes it the *perfect* design. We fall short of fulfilling that desire in our hearts when we try to find it in people or things. God alone is the complete fulfillment of every heart through a love that accepts us the way we are.

When we allow God's love to consume our hearts, everything pretending to be the love and acceptance we desire burns away. We begin to realize our infinite worth without any obligation to prove it. The proving was done by God through Jesus, and nothing else needs to be done. We're free to be who we are, and no one on earth has the okay to *not* be okay with it.

God's love shows us the way to believe in ourselves, exercise our gifts, and discover our unique purpose. Outside His perfect love is where we get lost in the endless pursuit of acceptance on the people-pleasing carousel. It will never satisfy our souls, and it will have us feeling less-than-enough most of the time. God's love for you is so complete, there's never a need to compete. You're valued beyond anything words can describe—and beyond the right of any person to decide.

Dear God,

Your love sets me free to be me!
Help me to know my worth is in
You alone and nothing else can
fulfill the desires of my heart.

A Promise from the Ashes

He will give: beauty for ashes; joy instead of
mourning; praise instead of heaviness.

ISAIAH 61:3 TLB

When the campfire is done burning and the embers have gone out and the ashes are all that remain of what was once a bright, beautiful, warming presence, it can hold a lot of comparisons to things we experience along the journey of our lives. We feel the happiness of wonderful things like the birth of a baby, the celebration of a wedding, birthday parties for the people we love, and memories we make with our family and friends. All are bright, beautiful, heartwarming, and irreplaceable.

Most of our journey can be likened to the embers that continue to glow after the flames disappear. The routine of the everyday is the foundation beneath the highlights and bright spots along the way. There's beauty there, too, that lasts long and keeps us warm. It inspires us to be thankful for the really good stuff and reminds us of God's *continual* goodness.

The ashes are symbols of the losses we suffer and the pain we walk through. Life is not without either of them for any of us. But in these seasons God is closest. When our hearts break, He brings the love and comfort we need to see us through our dark days. He brings another thing too. A promise that beauty will ignite from the ashes, joy will be rekindled and brighten our souls in a new, maybe deeper, way, and our hearts will one day feel like singing again.

Life changes constantly, but our peace is in the love that never does. God's love is the light for all the days of our journey, and there's nothing in this world that can ever diminish it.

Dear God,

Every part of the journey of my life is in Your hands. Give me strength to see that everything I go through is part of Your loving purpose for me.

The Cornerstone of a Simple Life

I have told you all this so that you will have peace of heart and mind. Here on earth you will have many trials and sorrows; but cheer up, for I have overcome the world.

JOHN 16:33 TLB

We can have a deep sense of peace today even if our lives are shrouded in uncertainty. God is still faithful. God is still good. God is still present. God is still working. Everything is being put into place to create a beautiful whole. Everything will fit together according to His plan, even when it seems the pieces are scattered in every direction.

It's a natural response to wish we could see what our lives will look like after the circumstances are weaved together for our good by the hands of God. Especially when the challenge appears insurmountable. God is bigger than any challenge and greater than any force of opposition. We don't have to know how it will work out; we have to stay strong and keep believing that it will. Maybe the reason Jesus told us to *"cheer up"* is because He knows joy is our path to strength—and we have to go to God to get the joy.

Peace of heart and mind is the cornerstone of living a simple life. If we try to stand strong under the weight of worry or we live in fear of outcomes we can't control, we set ourselves up for exhaustion. Our peace of mind is knowing everything that comes against us has been overcome by the love that saved us. And that love has the power to cheer us up in the face of *any* trial.

Dear God,

Stir up the joy in my soul for the strength I need today. Give me courage to trust the unseen working of Your hands and faith in knowing love will bring the best outcome.

Never be in a hurry;
do everything
quietly and in a
calm spirit. Do not
lose your inner
peace for anything
whatsoever, even if
your whole world
seems upset.

ST. FRANCIS DE SALES

Keeping Calm and Loving On

Step out of the traffic! Take a long, loving
look at Me, your High God,
above politics, above everything.

PSALM 46:10 THE MESSAGE

We've all seen or heard the phrase "Keep Calm and Carry On." Remaining calm is essential to maintaining the right response to anything or anyone. When we catch ourselves wanting to react hastily and harshly, we need to temporarily refrain from typing or talking and take a long look at how God would respond in the same situation.

"Love suffers long and is kind; love does not envy; love does not parade itself, is not puffed up; does not behave rudely, does not seek its own, is not provoked, thinks no evil; does not rejoice in iniquity, but rejoices in the truth; bears all things, believes all things, hopes all things, endures all things" (I Corinthians 13:4–7 NKJV). In every way, *God keeps calm*. We should, too, if we want our lives to be channels of love in a world desperately needing it.

Nothing should influence our actions more heavily than love. We're going to disagree with people about a lot of different things, but making our point will never matter as much as love does. Love matters most, and it truly is as simple as that. A life of simplicity keeps our minds and hearts in *love everybody* mode, never one that hangs on to offenses or holds out to make a point and prove we're right. We need only to make a point to step out of the hustle and bustle and stay focused on God's way, where love will *always* take the lead.

Dear God,

Let me be a channel of love to everyone in my life. Your love can change the world through the actions I choose and the words I use.

Taking Time to Restore Your Light

You are the world's light—a city on a hill,
glowing in the night for all to see.
Don't hide your light!

MATTHEW 5:14–15 TLB

The warmth of a campfire draws people in. The light and heat of it draws a lot of other living things, too, like critters and bugs! Knowing that God put His light in us is a powerful and humbling call to action. Even on days when we feel like shielding ourselves from attention of any kind, the hope we carry is a spotlight on God's love. It's a love everybody needs in whatever way we can give it.

On days when we're tired, feeling insecure in our readiness, or unworthy of the task of being a beam of sunshine, we need to refuel. And there's nothing wrong with taking the time to let God simply love on us. Do some things you love doing, things that will restore the brightness in your countenance. God put those needs in you and created you to enjoy them. They're not the same for any of us. You might need a hike or a bike ride. Someone else might need a good book and a cup of Earl Grey. And some of us love a long nap in a quiet house.

Reach out to the people in your life who are willing to help you brighten your spirit and bring your inner light out of hiding. It never goes away, but it needs encouragement now and then. God understands, and He loves the you He created. He knows exactly what you need today to get back your beautiful glow. Trust Him to give it to you in abundance.

Dear God,

I rest in You today and take time to soak up
Your love for me. Fill me with the comfort I
need through simple things I love and enjoy.

The Simple Truth of Grace

He has showered down upon us the richness of His grace.

EPHESIANS 1:8 TLB

The simple act of seeing a sunrise can shift our mindset for the whole day. It never fails to move us on a spiritual level. It brings an acute awareness of God's unfathomable goodness. It reminds us of the grace we walk in, a forgiveness and love so overwhelming it's hard to believe it's free. It's easy to fall into the trap of trying to prove we're good enough through our deeds, that we're worthy enough through our accomplishments, and that we're only acceptable through our appearance. God says otherwise, and Jesus proved that what God says is *true*.

God says, "There is nothing in the entire universe that can keep Me from loving you. And you're forgiven, for everything, and it won't cost you a thing. You don't have to earn an ounce of grace. It's a favor that not only covers you but carries you into My presence where you can get all the help you need to live a peaceful, purposeful, fulfilling, and victorious life."

Grace can feel like it goes against everything we know. The thinking that if we work harder and longer to buy bigger and better, we're "making" it. The belief that if we get

152

in the right shape and wear the right things, we're going to be more acceptable, more likable, and, sadly, more lovable. Again, there is nothing you can do to be more lovable to the One who created you in a wonderful, miraculous, and *amazing* way.

Wake up early enough to watch the sun rise every now and then—and remind yourself, to the depths of your soul, how worthy you are, how freely you're forgiven, and how eternally you're loved.

Dear God,

Thank You for loving me without a single condition. I'll walk through the day in the light of Your favor and forgiveness, feeling the deep sense of worth only You can give.

Living with a Childlike Trust

Whoever becomes simple and elemental
again, like this child,
will rank high in God's kingdom.

MATTHEW 18:4 THE MESSAGE

We can learn a lot about living a simple life from watching children. Buy them the most expensive toy on the market and they want to make a fort out of the box it comes in. They find endless, inexplicable happiness in rocks, dirt, sand, and water. It can't get more honest, innocent, or simple than the way children see things and say things, or more genuine than the way they question things. Curiosity is one of the simplest and most sacred qualities of a child, one that we as adults struggle to keep.

When we find ourselves forgetting to question why a flamingo's feathers are pink, why a rainbow follows the rain, or why the combination of chocolate and peanut butter is so perfect, it's time to spend some quality time with a child. One of the most admirable traits of a child is their willingness and ability to trust—and that's very likely the one God wants us to hold on to.

Trusting our heavenly Father without hesitation gets harder as we grow up. We're adults and we can take care of things. We know things and we like to control things. A simple, childlike trust is something we rarely practice, so we stop being good at it. God loves us so much that He allows some trust-building circumstances to come into our lives. He refreshes our childlike dependence on Him and shows how trustworthy, loving, and able He is to take care of us. Simple trust is the basis of a simple life—one filled with all the joyful and carefree days of a child.

Dear God,

Restore a childlike spirit in me and give me a renewed trust in Your perfect care.

A Simple Change in How We See

Every morning tell Him, "Thank You for Your kindness,"
and every evening rejoice in all His faithfulness.

PSALM 92:2 TLB

We all have morning rituals. It might be treating ourselves to something sweet and preferably chocolate with our coffee. It might be opening our eyes to two little eyes staring at us and waiting for morning snuggles. It might be stretching, breathing, and feeling thankful. Hopefully, we try to squeeze in some quiet time and simplicity. Fresh air. Seeing the colors of the morning sky. Listening to nature wake up for the day.

Small things in the beginning of our day have a lasting effect on us throughout the day. When we start by writing down a few things we're thankful for, or simply reflect on a few things we're thankful for, an appreciation for God's goodness seeps into our souls and lingers for a while. We notice things in our day that we usually take for granted. We pay attention to little acts of love from God, especially the ones that let us know He knows what we're going through.

A simple life isn't a major shift in how we do things as much as it is a change in how we see things. We have to look for God's hand in every part of our lives to know how *com-*

pletely He can be trusted. He can be, and He's constantly showing us. Every new day comes with a whole new set of ways God has planned to reveal Hs love and kindness to us. When we see and take note, He smiles and gives more.

Dear God,

I'm thankful every morning for the love

and kindness You give in generous,

personal ways. Open my heart and

mind today so I notice them all.

Stay Calm and Look Closely

God loves you very much . . . don't
be afraid! Calm yourself.

DANIEL 10:19 TLB

Calm mornings make us feel ready to go with a renewed energy, while chaotic ones feel like they sap the energy we need to get through the rest of the day. If things start with a rush, sneak away for a few minutes. Sit quietly and just breathe. Do a quick, simple reset. God sees how your day is going to unfold, and He's got some good stuff lined up. Remind yourself to look for it. It will sometimes come in small, unexpected ways.

Too much of the time we think routine leaves little room for the unexpected. But God's goodness is full of surprises. We can miss them if we're not looking in the ordinary places, in things we do every day. If we set our minds on being grateful and content, we welcome God's love in by way of the truth: "I have called you by name; you are Mine" (Isaiah 43:1 TLB). "You are precious to Me and honored, and I love you" (Isaiah 43:4 TLB). "I will care for you" (Isaiah 46:4 TLB). "I am with you always" (Matthew 28:20 TLB).

If we're going to live simple, content, and grateful lives, we have to keep our thoughts filled with simple truths about

God's unconditional love for us. It's not going anywhere, no matter what we do or don't do. Love expresses itself in kindness, care, and generosity. It holds on when we give up. It stays strong when we're weak. God's perfect love is going to show up today, and you're going to know it's meant just for you.

Dear God,

Help me see Your love in simple ways,

even in ordinary moments of my day. Fill

my thoughts with the truth about Your

true, persistent, and perfect love.

Don't Worry, Be Wild

*Let heaven fill your thoughts; don't spend your
time worrying about things down here.*

COLOSSIANS 3:2 TLB

A field of wildflowers can be more captivating and beautiful than manicured rows of flowers planted in a formal garden. Wildflowers just *are*, blooming happily wherever they land. They're not fussed over and they're not fussy. There are no expectations on them to grow neatly and upright. They simply reach for the sun, turning any direction they like. They are created by God to adorn our earthly home.

Wildflowers are a perfect example of how simple and carefree we should live our lives. So much so that Jesus put them in a parable.

"Walk into the fields and look at the wildflowers. They don't fuss with their appearance—but have you ever seen color and design quite like it? The ten best-dressed men and women in the country look shabby alongside them. If God gives such attention to the wildflowers, most of them never even seen, don't you think He'll attend to you, take pride in you, do His best for you?" (Luke 12:25–28 The Message)

You're beautiful just the way you are, and you're meant to be right where you are. Your gifts are God-orchestrated and heaven-sent. Use them to adorn your spot in the world with the unique colors that make you *you*. God made no mistake about the details of your design. You have lives to touch, love to give, and kindness to spread.

When the storms come, God's *got* us. We don't have to overthink, overwork, or overachieve. A simple life is the sweetest and surest life of all because we get to it by trusting God without a breath of uncertainty. We can only live it one day at a time, so let's put our whole hearts into beginning today!

Dear God,

All that I am is because of You. There is no
flaw in Your design. I praise You for making
me wonderfully complex and wildly different
from anyone else. Give me the courage
to live fully and freely in Your care.

Blessed at Home

And the homes of the upright—how blessed!
PSALM 112:2 THE MESSAGE

It always feels good to be home. Our lives are simpler there. We can breathe easy, be who we are, and express how we feel into a safety net of understanding. We're surrounded and supported by those who love us best and forgive us most often. Learning to love patiently and well starts at home, and it's a great way to get good at loving *all* the people God made. If we practice long-suffering, selflessness, kindness, and always looking for the best in people right in our own home, we're going to do far better at shining God's love into the world around us.

God shaped the families we have and provided the homes we dwell in. They're gifts we commit into His hands daily, while nurturing a deep appreciation in our hearts for all He's given. The world with its wars, trials, tragedies, and darkness is held at bay within the walls of our home. God is our comfort there, and He sees the needs both inside and outside it. The peace He brings calms us and gets us through the tough days and the difficult times. He's aware of it all, and nothing shakes the strength of His love or the hope it inspires.

Home is where campfires in the backyard are the ones we enjoy most and where roasted marshmallows taste better for some reason. Blessings begin here, abide here, and build a foundation for our dreams. When our hectic days roll into quiet evenings and bedtime prayers, it's good to pause. God is in these moments with a presence and love we can feel at few other times, in few other places.

Dear God,

Your blessings are abundant and keenly felt in the good things You've given. Thank You for being our dwelling place and for faithfully dwelling in the place we call home.

"Keep your
lives simple
and honest."

ZECHARIAH 8:17
THE MESSAGE

Stress Relief in the Simple Things

Smile on me, Your servant; teach me the right way to live.
PSALM 119:136 *THE MESSAGE*

The simple things are the best stress relievers. Things like taking a walk, watering the garden, watching the birds at the feeder, listening to a favorite playlist, the first sip of coffee in the morning, laughing with our kids, a drive through the countryside, and sitting around a campfire.

The pace of the world has complicated our lives and stolen our time with screens, apps, and binge-watching. When we think back just twenty years, it's shocking to realize where we are today in relation to the way we communicate and the things that monopolize our free time. And we have so little free time to begin with. Reclaiming it takes effort. To get back to the simpler, stress-relieving activities that are so *good* for us, we need to be deliberate about putting a whole bunch of things in our lives on "silent" more of the time.

God gives us the days; we choose how to fill them. "Whoever wants to embrace life and see the day fill up with good, here's what you do: . . . run after peace for all you're worth" (I Peter 3:10 *The Message*). We need peace and quiet. We need simple things. We need to make wise choices to make wider spaces for doing the little things that decompress us.

We have to look up, at each other, when we talk, dine, and spend time together.

God created us to cultivate *relationships*. If we get caught up in catching up on all the newsreels and television shows, we miss the things God wants us to see—people, even our own, who need encouragement, hope, and a hug, or the elderly person at the grocery store who needs a hand or even a second of eye contact to feel they're not alone in this world. Real people *really* matter. We can do with less screen time today. Let's look up. Let's be God's love. And let's spend time doing a few simple things that make us smile.

Dear God,

Give me the wisdom to spend my time putting people first. Show me how important it is to invest in simple things with a quiet, thankful heart.

Finding Quiet in the Clamor

He quiets the raging oceans and all the world's clamor.

PSALM 65:7 TLB

Let's never become accustomed to clamor. Instead, let's get back to bonfires, fishing, camping, and nature walks. Let's always hear the birds sing in the morning and listen to the tree frogs at dusk in the spring. Let's rest in knowing that God can quiet our hearts, too, so we never stop listening to Him, or to each other. There are so many *good* things that come from quieting the noise in our lives.

When was the last time you worked a little quiet into your day? We don't need huge chunks of time to get away from the busyness; just a few minutes can have a calming effect. We come away feeling refreshed enough to keep going. We're reminded how much we need silent pauses in our day. When we walk away from the text tones, voices, phone calls, and email alerts to sit for some quiet moments, it brings us back to our better selves. Things become clearer and God comes closer. He's in the quiet. He brings the peace. He knows the source of our stress, and He knows how to calm us. He knows *us*.

Being known is one of the most beautiful aspects of love. We don't have to explain what we need; God already knows what we need. We don't have to hope our questions are being heard and understood; God is already bringing the answers. It takes quietness to bring us back to the center of truth. God is our refuge, our shield, and our friend. He's our calm, our confidence, and our strength.

There isn't a moment of your day that isn't covered by the God who loves you, believes in you, and is *for you* no matter what. Get away from the noise and give everything to Him—He's well able to work out what is loving and best.

Dear God,

When I'm in the quiet times, be the One I hear

clearly. You are truth and light, and my heart

can rest in knowing You meet all my needs.

Simplifying to Strike a Balance

Wherever your treasure is, there your
heart and thoughts will also be.

LUKE 12:34 TLB

O rganizing our spaces is getting a lot of attention these days, and the wellness benefits of taking time to sort and simplify are selling a lot of books. It's for good reason. Simplifying is good for our souls, and it's wisdom God gave long before any books were written on the subject. He knows that what we spend the majority of our time working for and maintaining will in turn take a great deal of room in our heads and our hearts.

It's not that God doesn't want us to enjoy the fruits of our hard work or spend resources on the things we love to do. The secret is keeping a balance, and balancing has everything to do with what's going on in our hearts. We know when our hearts are consumed by things, and so does God. "So long as we are occupied with any other object than God Himself, there will be neither rest for the heart nor peace for the mind" (Arthur W. Pink, *The Sovereignty of God*).

Being "occupied" to the point of obsession or exhaustion is not God's best for our lives. He wants us to focus our time and energy on the things He knows will bring us fulfilling lives and eternal rewards. Stacking up and storing material possessions won't do that. It's amazing how clearing out and minimizing even one area in our homes or our lives can make us feel lighter, both physically and mentally.

A lighter heart and mind leaves more room for God to work through our lives. Nothing on this earth matters more. We aren't here long, and there are a lot of people longing to see the love of God. Let's pray for the chance to show them today.

Dear God,
Renew a clean heart and a right spirit in me, one that puts You first and keeps my life balanced and ready to show Your love and kindness to others.

It's Never Good to Get Ahead

Give your entire attention to what God is doing right now, and don't get worked up about what may or may not happen tomorrow. God will help you deal with whatever hard things come up when the time comes.

MATTHEW 6:34 *THE MESSAGE*

It's been said we should count each day a separate life. How simple would our days be if we took that to heart? The people we love would take priority. We wouldn't be anxious about the meeting next week, the bills coming at the end of the month, or the appointment we have tomorrow. Our focus would be squarely on today and what's in front of us right now. When God asks us to live in the moment, He's asking us to trust Him and take every thought captive to truth. We can't physically be anywhere *but* today. Our thoughts—aka worries—are what need to be wrangled into submission.

Fixing our thoughts on the now is more easily done when we fill our minds with the truth. "God is able to bless you abundantly, so that in all things at all times, having all that you need, you will abound in every good work" (II Corinthians 9:8 NIV). God is our unfailing provider. It doesn't matter what we need or how tall an order it is, God will meet it. All we have to do is keep our thoughts tuned in to His love for us and His faithfulness to us.

While we should never get ahead of God, it's good to think back. It helps us feel secure in the present when we reflect on the times God came through for us in the past. It's good to write those acts of love down so we can read them anytime we start to get anxious. Our worries are all a little different, but more likely than not, they're tied to things we can't see a solution or an end to. God wants us to remember that we never have to handle our days, our diagnosis, our debt, or our discouragement alone. It doesn't matter what our circumstances look like, God sees us, the answer, and the way through.

Dear God,
Give me the courage to stay in today. Let me live it with trust, a quiet mind, and a strong heart. Your love and provision are here.

Refreshed and Grateful

The LORD directs the steps of the godly.
He delights in every detail of their lives.

PSALM 37:23 NLT

Whenever we get some free time and feel a nudge to do a simple thing we love to do, we should get into the habit of doing it! God delights in our delight, and *every good thing* in our life comes from Him. It could be spending a little time at a nearby fishing spot. It might be planting flowers, working in the garden, walking through a boutique, going for a run, or listening to music. Maybe it's baking, painting, or looking for a new restaurant to try. Doing what we love to do is a way of appreciating and savoring God's goodness.

The things we enjoy doing reveal who we are in many ways. Each one of us is an original design. What makes our spirit soar and our heart happy is a part of how we're created, and it's as wonderfully unique as we are. When we do things that are fulfilling, that cultivate in us feelings of peace, relaxation and happiness, we feel refreshed and grateful to be *alive*.

Life is God's greatest gift to us. Our days come and go quickly. Simple joys slow us down a little and help us realize how much we have to be thankful for. When we rush through our days, we can miss things that God wants us to see and do. We miss opportunities to be His hands when someone needs help. Too many times we're looking down when we should be looking around—for opportunities to be kind, for ways to give hope, for chances to be a light, to share God's love, and to make an impact on someone's life.

We have the gift of today. Let's appreciate the simple things, slow down, look up, and pray that the people around us see a glimpse of God through us.

Dear God,
I'm thankful for every good thing You
put in my life and the time I have
to slow down and enjoy them.

The Sweetness of Sunshine

He shall be as the light of the morning; a
cloudless sunrise . . . as sunshine after rain.

II SAMUEL 23:4 TLB

Sunshine makes a day happier. It doesn't matter if it's a cold, cloudless day or a warm one with puffy white clouds and peeks of sunshine. When the sun is out, it makes everybody feel a little lighter. Even the birds sing more exuberantly. Sunlight has a way of lifting our spirits. We can all agree that a sunshiny day is one of the simplest, sweetest times to think about God's love, light, warmth, and kindness.

God's love within us is like sunshine to those *around* us. It lightens sorrow, brightens discouragement, and lifts weariness. The people God brings across our paths may not know the source of our light, but they'll remember how it makes them feel—and it will be God's love that makes their day. He sees hearts; we see faces. Every chance we have to shine into a difficult or dark place, we should. We never know whose heart is in need of a little sunshine.

There will be days when we don't feel like a bright yellow ball of light that's bursting with joy, and that's okay. We'll have emotionally cloudy days. We'll have stormy days when we're tossed and turned by what's going on in our lives. Those are the days when it's important for us to spend time basking in the truth that is *always* shining and *never* shrouded: "God is our Light and our Protector. . . . No good thing will He withhold from those who walk along His paths" (Psalm 84:11 TLB); "What a wonderful God we have . . . the one who so wonderfully comforts and strengthens us in our hardships and trials" (II Corinthians 1:3–4 TLB); "Let Him have all your worries and cares, for He is always thinking about you and watching everything that concerns you" (I Peter 5:7 TLB).

Whatever kind of day we're having, God's love is the only thing that makes a real difference through us or for us. It makes every day feel like the sun is shining.

Dear God,

Be the brightness in me that brings sunshine into the world. Fill me with the joy of Your presence and the love that brings hope. Let me be a light that leads every searching heart to You.

A Beacon of Hope

Feed the hungry! Help those in trouble! Then your light will shine out from the darkness, and the darkness around you shall be as bright as day.

ISAIAH 58:10 TLB

I n a grassy field covered in a blanket of darkness, a *single* firefly can be seen. No matter how vast the darkness, a tiny amount of light can pierce it like a beacon of hope. In our lives, light can be so many small, simple things. A kindness shown. A hand held. A neighbor helped. A friend hugged. A parent called. A child rocked. A note written. A prayer lifted. A meal delivered.

All we do from a place of love can change the darkness in this world. Nothing is more effective or meaningful. God's love is how light travels through us to get to the lives that need it. And if there's ever a time we need to be conduits of love, it's now! Spotlights, floodlights, flashlights, beacons, a candle, a match light, or a spark—every bit of light in any sort of capacity makes an amazing amount of difference.

We can go through our days thinking we don't have a minute to do another thing, but God is the strength and the supernatural power source we need to keep sending the love. There's no greater reward for our time. There's no deeper satisfaction for our souls. There's no better re-charge for our spirits. Love is what created us, and it's what we're created for. It's always the best way to spend our time and resources.

It's a new day to be a light in a small, simple way. What God opens our eyes to, we should open our hearts to do. His love is our shelter, our strength, and our reason to shine. How wonderful that we're chosen to dispel the darkness in any way that we can.

Dear God,

There's no deed too small to light our world with God's love. Every way eternally matters. The more You use me to make a difference, the more thankful I'll be.

The Single, Simple Thing to Do

Love each other just as much as I love you.

JOHN 13:34 TLB

Light helps us see. Around a campfire, glowing faces. With a flashlight, the path ahead. Under a streetlight, the rows of houses. Our lives help the world see the love of Jesus. Our actions illuminate the heart of God. What is He like? How would it feel to be in His presence? We can let the world know, because when we know how much He loves us, His light is what shines from us.

God's love is all we need to be who we are. It fills us with the confidence that we're doing exactly what we're created to do. It's never complicated. Love encourages a simple life of being like Jesus. He shared the love of God with openness, kindness, and compassion. His love welcomed everyone and excluded no one. He showed us what God needed us to see: loving people is the thing we should be putting first and doing most.

When our lives start to feel like they're getting chaotic, distressed, and unhappy, we're getting too far away from the single, simple thing God gave us to do: *love the people in your life*. Every relationship we have is one God is aware of and knew would happen. Nothing is by accident when God has been surrendered to, and that's the most peace-giving thing we can do.

Love should always look the same. "Love is very patient and kind, never jealous or envious, never boastful or proud, never haughty or selfish or rude. Love does not demand its own way. It is not irritable or touchy. It does not hold grudges and will hardly even notice when others do it wrong. It is never glad about injustice, but rejoices whenever truth wins out" (I Corinthians 13:4–6 TLB). In our homes, our workplaces, the grocery stores, or restaurants, love should look like God is the One giving it. It should light up the places He's chosen us to be.

Dear God,

Make my life a lighthouse of love. Fill my heart
and mind with the magnitude of love You
give to me every day, and grow my capacity
to love everyone in my life the way You do.

*Light a campfire
and everyone's
a storyteller.*

JOHN GEDDES

Defined by Contentment

Take care! . . . Life is not defined by what
you have, even when you have a lot.

LUKE 12:15 *THE MESSAGE*

What will you do with what you've been given? What brings you joy, and what are your gifts? You have many! God's love is generous, and He's given you much. A lot of us get caught up in believing our accomplishments have to be seen through a worldly lens of success in order to matter. We start to think that simple things are less important, so we put them off or let them pass. Things like touching base with a friend, sitting with an aging parent, helping a neighbor, visiting someone in the hospital, sending an encouraging letter, or taking time to listen.

Contentment is one of the highest forms of gratitude our hearts can give to God. What we have in our lives at this moment is what He's given, and it's more than enough. We have eternal things to affect right now, where we are, in the lives that we're a part of. Will God give us a wider reach in the future? If He does, *none* of it will be of *greater importance* than what He asks us to do today. We can't compare our lives with anyone else's; nor can we think that a simple life filled with small acts of service, continual acts of love, and a constantly content and grateful soul is worth less in God's eyes. Each of our lives is infinitely valuable. "There is no partiality with God" (Romans 2:11 NKJV).

Let's love others today to the fullest extent we can. Let's use the gifts God has given us to comfort, support, and strengthen someone in need right where we are. These are priceless ambitions that carry eternal rewards. Not one of us is more important than another, and every single thing God inspires our hearts to do is worth our attention, our time, and our very best effort.

Dear God,

I'm grateful for everything You've given me. I'm content to love others and invest in their lives, which is more valuable than anything else I can do.

Devoted to a Simple Work

Life is worth nothing unless I use it for doing the work
assigned me by the Lord Jesus—the work of telling others
the Good News about God's mighty kindness and love.

ACTS 20:24 TLB

If we begin to think that a simple life is less desirable or less fruitful than one driven by goals, guided by schedules, or measured by followers, it might be time to step back and reassess where we find our worth—and what is most worthy of the devotion of our hearts. There will never be a more worthy aspiration than sharing, showing, or being a shining example of God's love and kindness. And there will never be anything more joyful to Him than seeing us appreciate the simple joys He puts in our days.

Are we missing the beautiful song of the bright red cardinal in the morning? Have we watched a sunrise or sunset lately? Did we notice the calming rhythm of the spring rain shower or the colorful rainbow that followed it? God's love and kindness toward us are *everywhere*. The beauty of nature is like God waving His arms and saying, *Look! All of this is for you. Everything I've done and continue to do is for you. You are the joy of My heart—and I want to be the joy of yours.*

When we make our lives about God's love and kindness, both in giving and receiving them, our devotion is in the right place. We find joy and feel worthy because love is at the center of all we value and all we do. There's nothing ful-filling about complicating our days. What God puts in them and plans for them is all we need. Peace is found in simply trusting that our moments are mapped out by the One who loves us more than we can imagine.

Look for the love notes today. God's simple and countless ways of saying, "I love you with an everlasting love." Then let the love spill out on everyone around you in every way that you can.

Dear God,

Your kindness and love are abundant

and overwhelming. Help me see them in

everything You've created and given.

Resetting the Balance

I can't keep quiet about You. God, my
God, I can't thank You enough.

PSALM 30:12 *THE MESSAGE*

P art of the enjoyment of having a campfire is listening to the sounds it makes. The hissing, crackling, popping, and snapping are somehow soothing. The sounds hold our attention. We feel thankful for the time we have to sit, relax, and reflect. Our minds and bodies rest for a little while, distant from the rush and routine of our days.

Whatever pulls us into a peaceful mode is always a good thing. And whatever produces a quiet, calm, and thankful spirit in us is a *great* thing. It's the kind of thing we should commit to doing on a regular basis. Even when we don't necessarily feel like making the effort to create spaces to get out of our routine and enjoy some rest, in hindsight we're always happy we did. It gives us a chance to break from the rut and reconnect with God, which is the most restorative thing we can do.

Meditating on what God has done or is doing in our lives influences what people will hear when they listen to *us*. We want them to hear things that make them think about God's love and goodness. We want our words to bring joy, courage, gratefulness, and hope. We want them to know that they're loved, completely and without a single condition.

The time we put into restoring our souls and resetting the balance we need in our lives is vital. Somewhere amid the ongoing obligations and pressures of our days, it's important for us to make peace a priority. We need time to reflect and reconnect. We need time to cultivate a grateful heart. When we do, every part of our life comes into better balance, and everyone in our life can see and hear the difference it makes.

Dear God,
I ask You to stir a more grateful spirit in me
as I center my thoughts on You and make time
to do things that nurture peace in my life.

So Much More Than Okay

What I'm trying to do here is get you to
relax, not be so preoccupied with getting
so you can respond to God's giving.

LUKE 12:29–30 *THE MESSAGE*

How many times have we heard someone tell us, "*Relax. Everything will be okay*"? It's easier said than done, especially when our circumstances have us anxious and fearful. We know that everything will be okay because God is more than able to make it so and *always* faithful to do so. But we have a hard time feeling okay when the things we see are not okay. When we switch our thoughts to truth and trust, hope does the work of fighting our fear. "This trust in God, this faith, is the firm foundation under everything that makes life worth living. It's our handle on what we can't see" (Hebrews 11:1–2 *The Message*)

God will get us through. God loves us far too much to leave our side or our situation. He's in it with us and He sees what we aren't able to. His plan is to give us hope and comfort while He works everything together for the best outcome. On the other side, He sees us more confident in our faith and more courageous in our hope. The next time the things we see don't line up with what we know is true, we won't be so easily swayed. Every one of those good things marks the priceless progress God wants for us on our journey.

The most beautiful truth God wants us to stay mindful of is this: "No eye has seen, no ear has heard, and no mind has imagined what God has prepared for those who love Him" (I Corinthians 2:9 NLT). Everything is going to be so much better than okay—and there isn't a promise more life-giving or joy-creating than that.

Dear God,
When circumstances try to steer my thoughts,
give me the strength to trust You and stand on
the truth. Your love is all I need to see me through
to the good things You have prepared for my life.

A Good Place

How precious it is, Lord, to realize that You are thinking
about me constantly! I can't even count how many
times a day Your thoughts turn toward me. And when
I waken in the morning, You are still thinking of me!

PSALM 139:17–18 TLB

We're in a good place. No matter what today looks like, how full our calendar is, or how many hundreds of things it feels like we have to do, we're in a *really* good place. We're in God's thoughts. *Constantly.* We're in the protection of His love. *Continuously.* We're in the pages of His story. *Courageously.* We're in the palm of His hand. *Confidently.*

It should be so simple to live without care. It should be so easy to lay our worries at His feet and walk away, knowing He's offered to take them all. A simple life of trust is the most secure life of all, yet we struggle to live it. Maybe one of the ways to get there is by creating a little room in our day for glimpses of simple *goodnesses.* We can slow the go-go-go pace of our lives if we determine to do it. A whole lot of things we rush around to do can wait. The sense of urgency we live with is self-induced a lot of the time. We need time to sit confidently in the palm of God's hand and let Him calm us, even carry us. We don't have to figure it all out.

"Come to Me, all you who are weary and burdened, and I will give you rest. Take My yoke upon you and learn from Me, for I am gentle and humble in heart, and you will find rest for your souls. For My yoke is easy and My burden is light" (Matthew 11:28–30 NIV). We can learn from a gentle and humble heart filled with love for us. We can rest our souls by leaning on Him. We don't have to do it all. Today, we can make a few simple stops to see the certain presence of God in our lives. His love is sure to show itself strong.

Dear God,
Your constant love and attention
to every detail of my life is the peace
of my heart. Thank You for
reminding me that I'm always held
and You're always faithful.

The Simple Life We Crave

So here's what I want you to do, God helping you:
Take your everyday, ordinary life—your sleeping,
eating, going-to-work, and walking-around life—and
place it before God as an offering. Embracing what God
does for you is the best thing you can do for Him.

ROMANS 12:1–2 THE MESSAGE

It's the simple, ordinary things we do every day in the spirit of love, kindness, and compassion that become our true legacy. The ordinary becomes extraordinary when God's love and light pervade them, and the little things we do make up the greatest part of our lives.

We live in a world where technology is racing forward, conveniences are increasing, and everything we want or need is dropped at our doorstep. Our lives should be simpler than ever before, yet we feel increasingly fearful and stressed. The pushback will come by getting back. Getting back to backyard campfires, Sunday drives, hikes in the forest, and dinners around the table. Getting back to fewer screens and more conversations. Getting back to doing the things that make us feel connected to one another and realizing that the small moments filled with love are more important than promotions, power, and pedestals.

The telling part for each of us is how the simple joys make us feel. When we do something we love to do, or spend quality time with someone we love, stress loses its grip for a bit. Life feels lighter, easier, and more fulfilling. God is in the joy, the love, and the moments that make us feel grateful. He gives the simple, good things that we enjoy and look forward to. He gives us the people we love. He fills our life with good things—we just have to make the time and take the time to see and appreciate them.

That's the simple life we crave, and can have, a little more every day. It all comes down to transforming ordinary moments by paying attention, being present, and pampering ourselves once in a while. Look for the simple joys and God will always be there—to fill them with love and to fill you with peace.

Dear God,

You fill my life with good things, and I'm thankful for each one. Show me where I need to make room to bask in the simple joys that give my heart rest and restoration.

Starting Our Day in a Simple Way

I'm never out of Your sight. You know everything
I'm going to say before I start the first sentence. I look
behind me and You're there, then up ahead and You're
there, too—Your reassuring presence, coming and going.
This is too much, too wonderful—I can't take it all in!

PSALM 139:2-6 THE MESSAGE

There's wisdom in starting the day in a simple way by praying for courage to keep going, to keep hoping, and to keep our spiritual chins up for what's ahead. God cannot and will not fail us. A simple prayer strengthens our spirits and sets our steps on the right path. It isn't hard to ask God for help, but it's hard to do what we need to do if we don't get Him involved. He loves being a part of everything we do, and it's because He loves *us*.

With love guiding our steps, we stumble a lot less and make a difference a lot more of the time. God opens our eyes to things that might not be on our schedules but will make a greater impact than we could imagine in someone's life. A continuous dependence on His direction keeps us from taking turns He knows will be detrimental and leads us to places He needs us to be. Timing is critical, and His timing in perfect. Our life is blessed when we trust it.

We can be in the habit of scheduling our days from start to finish, thinking the best days are the ones that follow our plans without a glitch. But divine detours prove to be delightful interruptions. We often have a story at the end of the day about how we met an interesting person, how we were able to help someone in need, or why we ended up with extra time at home to make dinner or spend time with the kids. God knows how to make our days matter most. He's the wisest planner with the *best* results. His love shows. His light shines. His hope spreads. And the world heals, one *divinely directed* step at a time.

Dear God,
Put my feet on Your path today and give my
heart the wisdom to follow Your lead.

Kindnesses Magnify Love

Be kind to each other, tenderhearted,
forgiving one another.

EPHESIANS 4:32 NLT

A simple kindness can make a spectacular difference in someone's day. We don't realize how powerful the little things can be. We forget there's a *big* love behind them. A love powerful enough to touch hearts and transform lives. A love that makes everyone feel valued. A love so pure it can change our world one kindness at a time.

There is always a way to be kind to a person who needs to see God's love in the kindness we give. Kindnesses don't always need words. God wants our hearts to stay willing to do the work of His hands. The kindness in our actions will speak volumes about the love in Him. It's tenderhearted and forgiving. It's perfect and unconditional. It's every hope fulfilled and every desire satisfied. God's love is what every heart longs for and looks for in the darkness we face.

It never needs to be complicated. God has our day orchestrated perfectly; our hearts simply need to be tuned in. The one who needs the "lift" we can give will come across our path. The act of kindness that will make an impact on a life will present itself. We have all we need to give all God asks of us.

We can go through our lives peacefully, knowing God will not ask us to strive in order to prove His presence or His love. He'll bring the right opportunities and the right people in the perfect ways and at the perfect times. The more we learn His ways, the more freedom we walk in. It's a simple trust in knowing our steps are ordered, our gifts will be used, and our God will be glorified in every one of them.

Dear God,
In all that I do, I trust Your love will shine
through. I want to be a faithful expression
of Your heart and a diligent extension of
Your hands in this world every day.

A plain and simple
life is a full life.

PROVERBS 13:7 *THE MESSAGE*

Slinging the Stress

As pressure and stress bear down on me, I find joy in Your commands.

PSALM 119:143 NLT

It would be wonderful if we could hit a mental button that asks the question "How can we simplify this?" every time we face something that ignites stress in our lives. Since God didn't design our bodies to carry stress, He gave us plenty of ways to navigate our minds out of it. He says, *Give all your worries and cares to Me, because I care about you. Your worries won't add a single moment to your life (or a single solution to the problem), so watch how I take care of the birds, how I set the sun, and remember that the very hairs on your head are numbered. I know you. And I know the best way to take care of every detail in your life.*

A simple life has more to do with our trusting God than our ability to clear our schedule. We can be busy and not be burdened. We can have full days and hearts free of worry. We can have a litany of loose ends and unknowns and still go to bed without fear and sleep soundly. We do our part by letting God do His. We are enough just the way we are. We'll get enough done every day with the strength and time we're given. We'll find joy and gratefulness in the people we love, the homes we have, and the work we do.

Stress steals our peace and silences our joy. With it goes our light—the one that shines God's love into the world around us. If we can't trust Him completely, we can't serve Him wholeheartedly or reflect the wholeness of who He is. His love holds us securely, and it upholds the truth of *every* promise He's made. If we can start today by mentally slinging our stress into the net of His perfect love, we can free our minds and hearts to be His love to others. To surrender to God is to live our simplest life—one that brings the best rewards.

Dear God,

Take the stress I'm holding on to and fill me

with Your love and peace. Keep my focus

on You and off the things I can't control.

Living with a Carefree Air

The joy of the LORD is your strength!

Let's choose to live joyfully today! Joy is strength within us and light to those around us. While happiness is a feeling that comes and goes, joy finds its way from one soul to another. When it does, the heart it reaches may seek joy's true source—and there it will find God's true love. We have the privilege of carrying and sharing that love every day, and joy is one of love's most admirable and desirable traits.

There's something incredibly beautiful about a person who lives lightheartedly. The joy that strengthens them lifts their spirit and gives them a pep in their step and a carefree air. It's a good thing. It's a God thing. It's a thing we all need to make it through the tangle of our sometimes messy, sometimes overwhelming days.

Like every fruit of God's Spirit, joy comes by *believing*. We believe God loves us without having to prove our worth or perform our best. We believe God cares for our every need without overworking or overextending ourselves. We believe God will comfort and carry us through the deepest valleys and darkest storms in our lives. Joy is the steady current within us that assures us God is present, in control, and invested in our highest good.

If we could gather around a campfire with God, there would be *fullness* of joy! The conversations would be encouraging, enlightening, uplifting, and hopeful. The mood would be happy, relaxed, refreshing, and peaceful. We can tap into the joy God gives for the strength we need *every* day—and if we do, it will lift the cares of everyone around us too.

Dear God,

Your joy is my strength and a powerful way for others to see Your presence in my life. Give me the joy that can't be taken away, and let it be the light in me drawing hearts to You.

The Things We Shouldn't Miss

The basic reality of God is plain enough. Open your eyes
and there it is! By taking a long and thoughtful look at
what God has created, people have always been able
to see what their eyes as such can't see: eternal power,
for instance, and the mystery of His divine being.

ROMANS 1:20 *THE MESSAGE*

Sometimes in the darkest, loneliest times of our lives, God chooses a uniquely personal way to remind us He is near. If we look for Him in the simple things, we'll learn to see Him in everything. For some of us it might be spotting a favorite bird or seeing a favorite flower. For others it might be an unexpected conversation that brings the words we need to hear. And sometimes God wraps His love around us in the awe of a beautiful sunset. One thing is beyond any doubt—God is tender and thoughtful, and He's keenly aware of what we're going through.

There's no greater reason to slow down and live a simple life than to understand what we're missing if we don't. We miss the birds, the flowers, and the sunsets. We rush through conversations, dinners, and visits, missing the things God wants us to hear or *say*. We miss learning what makes our children laugh or what lights up their eyes and fuels their dreams. If we don't pace our lives to allow time for the simple things that bring us the deepest joy, we miss too much of what God has for us.

Everything He has for us is all about His love for us. It's an endless, powerful, unbreakable love that is ours without *any* condition. We can't run from it, no matter how fast our lives are speeding past. We can, however, change our pace and notice it more. God's love is not difficult to see or hard to find. He would never make it that way. It's here, right now, in every simple, good thing in our lives.

Dear God,

Your love is in every created thing and in the good things You want me to slow down to see. Make what's most important to You clearer to me every day.

LIVE YOUR FAITH

Dear Friend,

This book was prayerfully crafted with you, the reader, in mind. Every word, every sentence, every page was thoughtfully written, designed, and packaged to encourage you—right where you are this very moment. At DaySpring, our vision is to see every person experience the life-changing message of God's love. So, as we worked through rough drafts, design changes, edits, and details, we prayed for you to deeply experience His unfailing love, indescribable peace, and pure joy. It is our sincere hope that through these Truth-filled pages your heart will be blessed, knowing that God cares about you—your desires and disappointments, your challenges and dreams.

He knows. He cares. He loves you unconditionally.

BLESSINGS!
THE DAYSPRING BOOK TEAM

Additional copies of this book and
other DaySpring titles can be purchased
at fine retailers everywhere.
Order online at <u>dayspring.com</u>
or
by phone at 1-877-751-4347